THE FARMER'S KITCHEN

D0012273

The Ultimate Guide to Enjoying Your
CSA and Farmers' Market Food

Julia Shanks and Brett Grohsgal

Published by:
CSA Cookbooks, Inc
37 Tremont Street
Cambridge, MA 02139
www.csacookbooks.com
617-868-5995

Even' Star Organic Farm
48322 Far Cry Road
Lexington Park, MD 20653

BACK COVER PHOTOS
(From left to right)
    Socca Crepe
    Watermelon Salad with Citrusy Vinaigrette
    Tomato Soup with Garlic Scape Pesto

All photo credits: Julia Shanks, except:
Christine Bergmark: Photos of Winter CSA Share, Cherry Tomatoes, Winter Greens
Hershel Shanks: Photo of Brett Grohsgal and Julia Shanks:

© Copyright 2011-2012 Julia Shanks and Brett Grohsgal. The book authors retain
sole copyright to his or her contributions to this book. All rights reserved.

To our mothers
Roberta and Judith

who taught us how great food can be!

And to our fathers
Clifford and Hershel

who taught us the beauty of the written word.

Table of Contents

INTRODUCTION

We have written this cookbook to help farmers' market customers and CSA subscribers easily enjoy the diverse bounty of local farmers' crops.

Brett worked in restaurants for over 18 year, being the chef, the executive chef, or as a hustling line-cook in over 14 establishments. Foods as fresh and intensely flavorful as what his farm (Even' Star Organic Farm in Lexington Park, MD) now grows were almost never available. Then, he and his kitchen staff instead had to make do with chemically-intensive but flavor-deficient shipped produce. Now his farm customers eat infinitely better. It is glorious to be a seasonally-oriented farmer, growing traditional and cutting-edge foods in all twelve months of the year. His family is happy to grow organic and real tomatoes, real strawberries, real everything.

Julia met Brett when they cooked together at Restaurant Nora in Washington DC. She learned first-hand about the difference in organic produce and what it means to cook seasonally. She worked as a chef in 3 restaurants, and as a line-cook in many more. As a culinary instructor, she helped countless students really learn the differences between local foods and insipid out-of-season tomatoes. In her backyard, she grows vegetables 7 months of the year in her tiny urban garden.

We proudly disregard the absurd dogma that the US market only cares about uniform and cheap foods and is concerned not a whit for safety or for flavor. We grow and eat artisanal foods, "slow foods" in European terms, and Even' Star will never farm for distant markets where looks are paramount and where safety and flavor are not even important.

The incredible number of people who buy locally make our farming possible. You actively and tangibly support local growers. The passion

3

of Even' Star customers for outstanding foods gives us long lines at farmers' markets when our ripe heirloom tomatoes –ugly to see but oh, so wonderful to taste-- are pouring out of the fields. It is refreshing to so often hear loyal patrons describe our petite but intensely aromatic and sweet strawberries to newcomers: "Yes, they're small. But these are real berries, and the big ones have no flavor! We only buy small strawberries now!" Your devotion and willingness to spread the word about great local foods empowers farmers to focus on farming. You advertise and market for us by spreading the word about the great flavors and economic benefits of locally grown produce. The gifts that loyal customers bestow on farms are immeasurable, and we deeply thank you.

We also know that you are busy. You don't often have the time to make complicated meals. We have hence kept the recipes in this book on the fast side, or at least straightforward enough that you are not chained to a stove. We follow the classic Italian tradition: a few outstanding foods simply prepared usually taste much better than a host of mediocre ingredients blended with secret seasonings and complexity.

But our busy schedules also mean that we advocate taking the time, when you have it, to prepare some of farm foods for long-term use and storage. Salad dressings come to mind: these take only minutes to fix, keep for months in the 'fridge, and let you reach for a convenient, flavor-packed aid to a fast meal in the future. Canning is great, but many of us lack the time for such projects. For a quicker solution, we advise freezing a few containers of stewed tomatoes or puréed basil for winter use. High summer does not really last very long, but we can store a few treats for the frosty nights of autumn or the howling winds of January.

CSA — Community Supported Agriculture — is a new agricultural model built upon the relationship between farmer and consumer. CSA farms are partially or entirely supported by members who pay in advance for weekly distributions of fresh produce. By accepting the possibility that certain crops may do poorly or even fail, members share in the inherent risks of farming. This model demonstrates a commitment to the farmer, and it allows small farms to thrive in otherwise unfavorable market conditions. Given the alarming disappearance of farmland across the nation, more and more people are abandoning the supermarket and joining CSAs.

Farmers' markets have become the new best place to find cutting edge foods. From professional chefs to home cooks to food writers, farmers' markets are now the destination to find the most high-quality, diverse, and exciting vegetables, fruits, meats and cheeses. In contrast, supermarkets, even the high end ones, can never offer truly ripe and superbly flavorful produce.

But the amazing diversity of foods from local farms can be confusing. This cookbook is designed to help you navigate through newly discovered foods. We want you to understand what produce is available, how to choose truly ripe vegetables and fruits, and how to best to store them. Finally, a larder of great recipes is essential to best appreciate what the farmers have grown for us.

We thank all of our customers for supporting local farms. You are the people that will let progressive American farms thrive in the 21st century. You make possible our stewardship and environmental goals.

We acknowledge that recipes are in the public domain once printed. We encourage you to use and share these recipes most freely. We ask nonetheless that you credit the source, CSAcookbooks.com, when and if you copy or distribute any recipes from this cookbook.

Thank you for supporting local farmers!

Julia Shanks and Brett Grohsgal
March 2012

CHAPTER 1: Eating Seasonally

No matter where you live, eating seasonally and locally offers a different way of thinking about food. While some areas of the country are relatively blessed to have locally grown fruits and vegetables for longer seasons, such as California and Florida, even these regions still have strong seasonality as to when each type of produce is at its best.

By contrast, other parts of the country have exceedingly short seasons, where summers seem like spring by New England standards; places like Minnesota and the Dakotas. In these regions, consumers face much greater challenges when it comes to eating fresh produce seasonally and locally.

Eating seasonally can indeed be a challenge – especially now that we can have anything we want anytime by heading to the supermarket. But making the effort to rise to that challenge can be a source of great satisfaction. Eating locally engages our powers of creativity, learning, and experimentation. Who would have guessed that fresh kohlrabi and okra could please so many grown-ups, that greens and sliced turnips right out of the fields could so easily draw kids away from packaged snacks?

Perhaps most important for us as food lovers, eating seasonally is glorious. Biting into the first ripe apple of the season, where the flavors perfectly match those of a crisp autumn evening, has made us stare at that apple in awe.

There are few greater joys than incredible tomatoes grown in your backyard or from a nearby farmer, brought to perfection by hot, sweltering sun. No shipped tomato, with their cardboard texture and insipid taste, can ever compare with the summer jewels. Cold-grown salad greens, traditionally the first crop harvested after the bleak winter, have exponentially more flavor, texture and excitement than shipped generic salad mix.

Of course locally sourced and seasonally raised foods taste better. They spend more time in the fields ripening – developing sweetness and flavor – because they don't need to be picked under-ripe for shipping thousands of miles away. Picking under-ripe vegetables also reduces the nutritional value. Farmers can grow more diverse varieties, bred for quality and flavor rather than long shelf life. And though a region may experience a drought or unusually cold weather for a season, the fruits and vegetables still grow at their optimal time, ensuring the best possible taste. Picking under-ripe vegetables reduces the nutritional value.

Buying local also benefit the environment and economy. When we reduce our "food miles," the distance our foods travel from farm to table, we reduce our carbon footprint – the impact of transportation, refrigeration and packaging needed to carry produce around the country. With each local food purchase, you ensure that more of your food dollars go to the farmer and local economy in the form of revenue and taxes. Buying local food keeps your dollars circulating in your own community. In Massachusetts alone (where Julia lives), if every household purchased just $12 worth of farm products for eight weeks (basically the summer season), over $200 million would be reinvested in our local farmland.

When you buy local, you help to ensure our farms survive for many years to come.

CHAPTER 2: Produce Descriptions

These general descriptions are intended to help you understand the flavor profiles and culinary uses of many vegetables and fruits you will find in the farmers markets and CSA boxes. No single farm grows all of these foods, and there are thousands of varieties that in the interest of space we cannot list here.

Apples

A favorite fall fruit, ideal for cooking or snacking. They make a bright addition to a salad with dried cranberries, walnuts and/or cheese. Refrigerator storage helps them maintain their texture, though they can handle a few days on the counter.

CRISPIN

Good eating apple, first-class cider and sauce. Green fruit ripens yellow.

FUJI

Crisp, juicy and slightly acidic. It has white flesh with outstanding texture.

GALA

A versatile apple, it's good for baking, in pies and snacking. Gala apples have pinkish stripes on yellow skin. This variety is very sweet.

GINGER GOLD

This variety has a sweet-tart flavor, good for pies, sauces and eating. It is an early apple, available in August or September.

GOLDEN DELICIOUS

Mild sweet flavor, juicy, crisp, light yellow flesh. It's not as tart as other varieties and holds its shape well when baked.

GRANNY SMITH
Tart with the best texture for baking and sauces. Across the globe, it's the #1 all-purpose apple for eating and baking.

HONEY CRISP
This is a new variety of apple, which was introduced in the early '90s. The skin color is a combination of red and yellow. It is not well-suited to baking.

JONAGOLD
Available in September, this variety is perfect for making pies and sauces with its balanced sweet-tart flavor.

MELROSE
Firm and quite coarse in texture, this apple's creamy white juicy flesh is slightly acidic in taste and actually improves with age.

RED DELICIOUS
The skin color of this variety of apple is red and has a very sweet taste. Mostly just an eating apple, though you could bake with it.

STAYMAN/WINESAP
Firm texture with a sweet-tart taste. It's a great all-purpose apple – for eating, baking and sauces. It's available in October.

Basil, all types
One of the treats of high summer cooking and salads, with very unique flavors treasured by cultures around the world – from Italy to Vietnam. It's best not to cut basil until just before serving as the leaves will blacken quickly. If using in a curry or stew, add a few sprigs in the beginning of cooking and a few leaves at the end for a bright pop of flavor and color. On a hot, summer day, a Basil Gimlet is a wonderful thing.

Beans (pole, snap)
Pole beans are named for the trellises on which they grow. When young and tender, they can be eaten whole. As they grow larger, they should be shelled, and the only the beans eaten. Fresh young beans are so naturally sweet, they need minimal cooking… They can be steamed for a minute or two, just enough to turn them bright green.

Beets
Beets sadly receive a bad reputation from the olden days when they were

always served mushy from a can. Fresh beets evoke a cult-like following because of their sweet, earthy flavors. Both the green tops and the roots are edible. The greens can be cooked similarly to Swiss chard or kale. Beetroots can be served raw if sliced thin like Carpaccio. More often they're cooked until tender by roasting, boiling or sautéing. They can be peeled before or after cooking, but waiting until after they cook provides a good indicator of when they are, in fact, cooked as the skins will peel off easily. Once cooked, peel them with a paring knife or peeler and cut. You can add them to salad, or season them simply with vinaigrettes.

Beets stain easily. To clean hands and cutting boards, wash them with baking soda and cold water.

Blackberries

These fragile berries taste best at room temperature, but must be stored in the refrigerator. High in anti-oxidants, they are great for snacks, or cooked in a cobbler or pie.

Blueberries

They have a sweet taste when mature, though the smaller berries tend to be more tart. Ideal for snacking, for topping cereal, or mixed into pancakes or muffins. Mixed with cinnamon and lemon zest, they make an ideal summer dessert.

Broccoli

Often a favorite vegetable for kids because of the tree-like appearance. Fresh broccoli is sweeter than the commercial varieties. Wonderful steamed, sautéed, stir-fried or just eaten raw as part of a crudite platter.

Brussels Sprouts

Brussels sprouts look like tiny green cabbages. They are best after the first frost when the flavor sweetens. Our favorite way to prepare them is simply roasted in a 400°F oven until golden brown, seasoned with olive oil and salt.

Cabbage
GREEN OR RED

Often thought of as a low-brow vegetable, cabbage's stature has been elevated as chefs have taken to serving it with more refined ingredients like lobster and truffles. Classically served raw in slaws, green cabbage makes a great addition to Chinese stir-fries or fried rice. Simply braised or stewed in tomato sauce, it also works well as a side to grilled sausages or fish. Red cabbage can be blended with white cabbage for slaw, or even used entirely on its own. Braised red cabbage (with red wine, vinegar and a little sugar) makes a wonderful accompaniment to hearty winter meat dishes.

CHINESE
These varieties requires less cooking time by far than Western style cabbages. They also may be cut up raw in salads. Whole heads can be halved (washed again), briefly marinated and grilled.

Cantaloupe
Sometimes not as sweet as other melons, cantaloupes pair well with blueberries, mint and ginger. A fully ripe cantaloupes is soft, very sweet and musky (remember its other name, muskmelon) Serve plain for breakfast, or as an appetizer with prosciutto. Cantaloupe puréed into a soup is a refreshing first course to a summer meal.

Carrots
With really fine carrots, peeling is not necessary, though some people find the outer layer slightly bitter. Be sure to wash them once more. The large ones are often more tender (best for raw); the smaller perhaps best for gentle simmering or glazing in honey and butter.

Cauliflower
Though the leaves are edible, most people eat just the white florets. The florets tightly grip a tough core in the center. Cut the cauliflower in half to expose and cut out the core. Cooked cauliflower does not last long in the refrigerator but can be easily frozen for longer storage.

Celeriac
Celeriac is a variety of celery with small stalks and is grown for its root. The celery root has a fuzzy skin that needs to be peeled before cooking or eating. It has a mild celery flavor with a hint of turnip, and can be used in place of (or mixed with) potatoes for mashed or gratins. Thinly sliced, it can be served raw, and tossed with mayonnaise for the traditional French rémoulade, a variant on coleslaw.

Celery
Though rarely cooked on its own, celery's distinctive flavor enhances French, Chinese and southern cooking. Its crunchy texture makes it a staple in egg, chicken or tuna salads.

Chervil

A classic French herb with a delicate flavor akin to a blend of nice parsley with sweet fennel. Outstanding in salads, or added late to sautéing chicken breast or white-fleshed fish. Makes an elite Dijon-based salad dressing. Heating past 210°F destroys most of the flavor.

Cilantro

An herb many people adore and a similar number cannot abide. We use it in salads, salsas, marinades for grilled shrimp and rockfish, and of course in many Thai dishes, Chinese soups, and with vegetarian bean-and-rice burritos. Heating past 190°F kills most of the flavor.

Corn

POPPING

Popping corn comes from a starchier variety than the sweet corn. Its tough outer skin traps just enough moisture to pop the corn into a low-fat, highly satisfying snack.

SWEET

Corn is one of the most cherished summertime crops for its sweet and crunchy flavor. Corn's sugar converts quickly to starch, so it's best to eat the corn as soon as you can. Boiling whole ears is perhaps the easiest way to prepare it: Put corn in a pot of boiling, salted water -- after the water returns to a boil, cook just for 2-5 minutes. It can be grilled in or out of the husks, or cut off the cob and sautéed in butter.

To wipe silk off an ear of corn, rub with a wet paper towel. To cut kernels off the cob, lay the ear on its side and run a sharp paring knife straight down the sides. Then scrape with the back of the knife to extract the very sweet "milk."

Cucumbers

Small cucumbers are crisper, rarely peeled, and are most convenient for snacking. Cut lengthwise and dipped in soy sauce, they can tempt even the most stubborn child. Small cukes are traditionally sliced and marinated with onions, sugar, dill and cider or white wine vinegar. Medium cucumbers are the most versatile but can become bitter in the scorching days of August. Bitterness in any size can be obviated by peeling and then soaking in water for about 5 minutes before slicing.

We prefer mediums to the other sizes because they need no de-seeding and you can do practically anything with them. They are fine for snacks, salads, cold soups, nori-roll sushi, etc., and are the best size for slicing and immersing in yogurt mixed with herbs. Larger cucumbers are usually the sweetest but often need peeling. Their large and juicy seed cavity is often discarded, especially if making gazpacho or other soups. Just peel, cut in half lengthwise, and scoop out the seeds and pulp with a tsp or melon-baller.

Dill

Home-grown dill has superior and balanced flavors relative to commercial herbs. Excellent in cold bean salads; in salads of greens, potato, cucumbers, or egg; mixed with sour cream for baked potatoes; in omelets; with dips for vegetables or in lemon-juice salad dressings; or with cooked fish or chicken dishes, added late. Heating past 210°F destroys most of the flavor, except when baked into breads.

Edamame (Soy Beans)

Traditionally, the whole pod is simmered with salt, beer and ginger for 10 minutes, or until the pods are bright green. Chilled, and beans popped out, they make a great snack. Once shelled, they can be added to a succotash or other summer salad.

Eggplant

Eggplant is a superbly malleable vegetable. It takes on the flavors of any meat or broth or seasoning you add while cooking, and offers an almost meaty feel to the palate. Different eggplant varieties present an amazing spectrum of firmness, bitterness, mild flavors versus strong, seediness, and propensity to melt (in contrast with staying firm) upon lengthy cooking. Japanese, Chinese and Italian varieties are favored for their mildness and tender skins. Eggplant should be stored on the counter until ripe, then refrigerated (refrigerating too soon can lead to small brown streaks in the flesh). The sweetest and most mild eggplants are permitted to ripen at room temp until they soften and slightly wrinkle. Like a peach, this softening and wrinkling means you've handled the eggplant perfectly, and you now need to use within a day or refrigerate.

The jury is still out as to whether salting eggplant before cooking reduces any bitterness. Without doubt, however, salting it for 15 minutes before cooking prevents the eggplant from absorbing oil when sautéing or frying.

Fennel Bulbs

Fennel is another lover of cool and relatively moist conditions. In truth, it really wants to grow in the mild springs of Italy and California. The bulbs ought to be separated into individual petioles (the pale green-white fleshy things that subtend the leafy parts, similar to celery). The petioles and tops should then be washed. Both are very usable, but with slightly different applications. The leaves are outstanding minced and added to bread or pizza dough before cooking, or minced and added to salads or salad dressings. The stems can be cut into ¾-inch pieces and barely simmered, with garlic and butter added late. And the most tender petioles are really fine served separated and raw but whole, smeared with nice soft cheese or butter. Alternately, use any recipe for the classic Italian dish of braised fennel, which uses the entire thing, cut up.

Fennel also pairs beautifully with tomatoes and seafood dishes like paella or bouillabaisse.

Garlic

Garlic can have a strong bite when raw, but mellows with cooking. To roast garlic: toss peeled cloves with 1 – 2 Tbs olive oil. Wrap in an aluminum foil pouch. Bake at 350°F for 25 minutes, or until the garlic smells sweet and is a light, golden brown. Even though it won't look burnt, garlic tastes bitter when it is cooked to a dark, golden brown.

Your hands may pick up the smell of garlic after chopping it. To remove the odor, rub your hands on stainless steel (the bottom of the sink is good) under cold-running water.

Garlic Scapes

Plants want to reproduce. Such is the case with hard-neck garlic. They send up slender stems with a flower bud at the end. Before the flower opens, we nip that urge to procreate in the bud–so to speak–and redirect the plant's efforts to its growing downward The stem and bud are known as the garlic "scape," They are a rare treat. Mild but seductively scented of garlic, they can be cooked any number of ways: served all on their own, or as an aromatic. They are most tender when picked before the stems begin to curl, although many varieties have tender scapes even in the fully curled state.

Green Beans/String Beans

Only snip off the stem end, the other is quite tender and creates a lovely presentation. Brief cooking helps to lock in the bright color and crisp texture. Longer cooking changes the flavor drastically to sweet and slightly tangy, which many Southern cooks prefer. The texture is then soft and the color is, unfortunately, not as vivid.

Greens

ARUGULA

Pungent and nutty, sometimes as hot as cress, arugula is unique in the greens world. Use and appreciation of this green has spread wildly across the US, but many remain who do not know it. The peppery leaves can be served on their own in a salad, mixed with other leaves for a lively salad blend, or even sautéed. Outstanding salad uses for arugula are with pears or apples, or mixed with romaine, sweet red peppers or boring out-of-season tomatoes. It is traditional and superb to use this in sandwiches paired with Brie, Camembert, chèvre, prosciutto, turkey, ham, or roast beef. For those who can't handle the pungency raw, arugula is wonderful in garlic-enriched broth soups or briefly cooked with other greens.

BOK CHOY

Sweet and tender. Diced, it makes a nice addition to salads. When harvested in the more mature state, it's very good sautéed with ginger, garlic, butter and dark sesame oil. When sautéing or grilling, try to use the succulent juicy white part in the hottest part of the pan or grill. Brief cooking keeps the stems and leaves most flavorful and crisp. Can be used like celery stalk as a hors d'oeuvre, spread with cream cheese or goat cheese.

COLLARDS

Collards are in the same family as broccoli and cabbage. The thick leaves can withstand long-simmering to tenderize them. While many Southern cooks will braise them for hours, 15 – 20 minutes is sufficient. The smaller leaves only require a quick cooking, and can rival spinach in supple texture and delightfully mild flavors.

CRESS

Cress, hot mustards, and horseradish share the extreme end of the pungency spectrum. Most mild of these (typically) is watercress. But all varieties grow more pungent as the growing temperature rises. Raw uses are in sandwiches (especially with cheeses) or mixed with more mild greens in salads. Cooking really tones down the pungency, and the cresses add great depth and flavor in soups.

FRISEE

A curly lettuce with whitish, pale green leaves. It has a nutty flavor that is mildly bitter. It can be mixed in with other lettuces to brighten up and give body to a salad blend. Its hardy texture allows it to stand up to brief cooking – grilled, in traditional soups of the Provence, or wilted in a warm salad.

KALE

Smooth kale is sweet and really tender. Curly kale has more body and more chew, so it is superior for hearty soups or to add plate height to other sautéed greens. Lauded for its great nutritional value, kales are very rich in vitamins and minerals.

LETTUCE

Little is more joyous than a delicate, crisp salad made with locally grown lettuces. Expect sweeter flavors when growing temperatures are cool, bitter when growing temperatures are hotter. Often requires one more washing.

MESCLUN

Mesclun is a blend of young leafy greens. The traditional mix includes chervil, arugula, leafy lettuces and endive in equal proportions, but in modern iterations may include an undetermined mix of fresh and available lettuces, spinach, arugula, Swiss chard, mustard green, frisée, sorrel, and/ or other leafy vegetables. Mesclun is good up to 5 days in a plastic bag. It should be washed and blotted dry just before using. The name comes from the Provence (Southern France)—mescla, "to mix"—and means "mixture".

MIZUNA

Frilly mild green, best for salads. Pairs nicely with Winesap apples or really good pears with a nice balsamic and olive oil. Also works well in sandwiches.

MUSTARD GREENS

The leafy greens of the mustard plant, these have a spicy, horseradish flavor and hearty texture. Brief cooking greatly reduces the pungency. Excellent in vegetarian bean dishes or with pork or beef. Sauté with pine-nuts, garlic and raisins to balance the flavor; this can be used as a side dish for to grilled meat or fish, or as a stuffing for chicken. Eat most varieties raw only if you are a lover of wasabi or horseradish.

PAK CHOI
These look like tat soi but are more pungent (mustardy) in flavor. They add a nice bite to sandwiches and salads, and they totally tone down when cooked. As versatile as tat soi and bok choy.

SORREL
A leafy green that is considered more an herb than a vegetable. The smaller leaves have a fruity taste and are better for eating raw. The larger leaves can be quite acidic, and can be added to soups or sauces for a bright flavor. Tart, citrusy and a must-have for many great French dishes. Sorrel is often puréed in soups.

SPINACH
Wonderful when grown in the cooler months. Wash thoroughly: fill a large bowl or sink with cold water. Add the spinach and swish it around a little. Let the dirt settle to the bottom, and then lift the spinach out to let drain in a colander. Superb raw. If cooking, cook just until wilted (about 30 seconds).

SWISS CHARD
Superb silky texture makes it one of the finest of all cooking greens. Best to cook the chopped stems longer than the leaves. You can add the stems to your cooking vessel about 1 minute before the leaves.

TAT SOI
Tat soi is really versatile: mild, tender, and nice in salads, sandwiches, steamed, in soups, sautéed, whatever! Keep and use the midrib and petiole (the white stem-like thing) on for its sweet succulence. The whole crown is even grill-able.

Jerusalem Artichokes
The root of a sunflower plant, it has little relation to the Italian artichoke plant. It garners its name from the flavor resemblance. Some say the flavor is closer to a nutty potato. It can be cooked like a new potato, but is less starchy. They boast a very high iron content – comparable to red meat - making them ideal for a vegetarian diet. We do not recommend peeling as it is too laborious and the skin is thin. Instead, scrub well under running water with a soft brush.

Jerusalem artichokes have a reputation for being, ahem, windy. To counteract this affect, store the tubers in the refrigerator for at least one month. In addition, they can be pre-cooked in boiling water for 10 minutes. The water should be drained and discarded. Once pre-cooked, they can be finished by baking, roasting, or boiling in fresh water.

Kohlrabi

In the brassica family, kohlrabi has an edible bulb that grows above the ground. The flavor is similar to broccoli stems. After it's been peeled, it can be eaten raw, sliced thin in salads, or sautéed in butter with garlic. It can also be used in Southeast Asian recipes as a substitute for green papaya.

Leeks

Superbly versatile in cooking and a required ingredient in many French soups. It's larger and sturdier than a spring onion. The white and pale green parts are eaten. The dark greens tops are sometimes too tough, though the tough parts can be used to flavor broths if they are strained out before eating.

Because of their shape, leeks trap a lot of dirt. They should be cut before washing to best release all the dirt. Soak them in cold water, the dirt will settle to the bottom, and the leeks should be lifted out before draining. Properly washed, they are also wonderful sliced in half lengthwise, simmered until soft, (chilled, if desired) and then tossed with vinaigrette.

Mint

Given its prolific growth, it's a good thing mint is so versatile – from desserts to grilled meats to drinks. Toss a few leaves with berries, steep leaves in hot water for tea, puréed for a sauce for lamb or salmon, or mixed with cucumbers or peas for a refreshing salad. It even brightens up a gin and tonic on a hot summer afternoon.

Mushrooms, Wild

Lucky indeed is the farmers' market customer who can buy wild mushrooms. We strongly advocate washing mushrooms, despite conventional wisdom against it. Growing on the forest floor means lots of grit and pine needles, and these can ruin the most delectable meal. Wash mushrooms as we advise for leafy greens. Drain well.

CHANTERELLES

Deeply floral aromas make this second only to the truffle in our passion. More gritty than other varieties; washing is critical. Superb with cream. Use low to medium heat when cooking.

19

HONEYS

They are close kin to the shiitake. With a clean, woodsy flavor, they are less thick and rubbery. They are best sauteed quickly over high heat. They don't store well; use quickly.

MORELS

The most woodsy of all wild mushrooms. Its bizarre, conical shape easily distinguishes it from other mushrooms. Without doubt, best sautéed slowly with cream.

OYSTERS

Mild, meaty and versatile. These have superior shelf-life compared to most wild mushrooms. Use in place of button mushrooms for outstanding flavor. Great in omelets and pizzas.

PORCINI

Porcinis (Cepes) are unique and very expensive mushrooms. Chefs and consumers forgive its most poor shelf life because of its perfectly nuanced flavors. Outstanding grilled, but adds an oyster-like texture to sauces when sauteed. Amazing (though pricey) in mac-n-cheese.

PUFF BALLS

They are the most mild of the wild mushrooms, like tofu. Best peeled and marinated before cooking to absorb more flavors. The bigger ones can be sliced and grilled, the smaller are nice mixed with other mushrooms.

Nectarines

Nectarines are, in fact, a variety of peach, and differ only in the fuzz-less skin. The fruit should smell sweet and "peachy" when ripe. While peaches and nectarines have a slight give when ripe, you don't want to test too often this way as they will end up bruised.

Okra

Okra is a much-maligned vegetable that we treasure sliced raw in salads, stewed, or deep-fried. Really fresh and tender okra is as delicate in flavor as baby green beans. The uses are many, from barely steamed, then shocked and chilled and finally dressed with vinaigrette; to deep-fried; to stewed. Raw and sliced 1/6" thick into summer tomato salads, it adds great sweet crunchy contrast as well as pleasantly thickening any vinaigrette.

Onions
DRY SKIN

Also referred to as "storage onions," they need not be refrigerated. They are a staple of all types of cooking. There are many tips to avoid tearing up when cutting, though none is fool-proof. The best solution is to use a sharp knife and cut quickly to minimize the exposure time. Better yet, have someone else cut the onions for you.

GREEN AND SPRING

Tend to be sweeter than storage onions, but should definitely be stored in the fridge to maximize shelf life. Excellent raw in salads or peeled and simmered whole. The big bulb onions can be cut in half or grilled whole, depending on their size.

Oregano
A common seasoning in both Mexican and Mediterranean cuisines, its flavor is a blend of mint, thyme and camphor. Some varieties have a slightly peppery/spicy taste. It is similar to marjoram, but less sweet and more pungent. It pairs well with other strong herbs and flavors: rosemary, thyme and sage; with potatoes, and meats.

Parsley
Mild, with a slight carrot flavor, parsley brightens most dishes with a sprinkle at the end. It's an essential ingredient when making soups and stews and adds a subtle backdrop of flavor.

Parsnips
They resemble carrots in their shape and they grow in the ground. But these sweet root vegetables have a flavor all their own. They must be peeled before cooking. Roasting brings out their sweetness, but they are also good boiled or mashed. You can use them in any recipe that calls for potatoes. The really large ones (about 2-inches in diameter at the widest point) will be tougher.

Peaches
Most of peaches' nutrients are in the skin. Washing them in cold water rids them of the fuzz. Nonetheless, many dessert recipes suggest peeling as the skin will fall off during the cooking and is considered unappealing. To peel a peach, score the bottom of the peach with a sharp paring knife. Put them in a pot of boiling water for 30 seconds. Scoop them out and plunge them into an ice bath to stop the cooking. The skin will now easily peel off.

Peas
ENGLISH

Anyone who does not like peas surely never had a sweet English pea fresh in the springtime. Sautéed in butter or tossed with mint, they are a refreshing side dish to lamb or salmon. They also work well in pasta dishes tossed with Parmesan and a little bacon.

SNOW, SUGAR SNAP

Oh, what joy a sugar snap pea is! Best de-stringed by snapping and pulling on the stem end gently. Excellent raw or very briefly cooked (no more than 30 seconds).

Peppers
SWEET · GREEN

Green peppers are excellent counterpoints when used raw in salads or crudites. Cooked, they add character to stir-fries, pastas dishes, but shine most brightly when braised, Italian style, with pork sausage or other meats.

HOT

Either you love them or you hate them. To most safely handle, wear protective gloves. Chop raw peppers and store in a glass container, covered with vinegar. They will keep indefinitely if refrigerated. Then when you want to add some welcome heat to a dish, use a spoon and spare your fingers.

The hottest part of the pepper tends to be the white membranes, and the seeds are second (though this can vary by variety). Remove these parts to create a milder heat in your recipes. Be careful not to touch your eyes or any other sensitive area after handling. Washing your hands with baking soda and cold water also helps to neutralize the burn.

SWEET · RED

Best all-around pepper for raw, dicing in salads, or stuffing and baking. To roast and peel red peppers, carefully blacken skin under an oven broil or over an open flame. Remove from heat, and place in a bowl. Cover with plastic wrap or damp cloth. Let cool and then the skin will easily peel off. These can be stored packed in olive oil in the freezer indefinitely, or in the fridge for 10 days or more.

ELONGATED · MANY TYPES

The US is going through a pepper revolution, with countless heirloom and new varieties now available. Most of the long types have richer pepper flavors than the classic bell. Some have no heat (like *Jimmy Nardello*), others have a touch or more (like *anchos* and *poblanos*). These long peppers are often best for cutting up and adding superb flavors to other dishes, or as focal points for sauces and relishes (e.g. Romesco, page 256).

Plums

The flesh of the plum is quite sweet while the skin is tart, giving this stone-fruit a wonderfully balanced flavor. It's a versatile fruit that can be dried for prunes, fermented for wine, or baked into tarts and pies. Plums can be substituted for any recipe that calls for peaches.

Potatoes ("Irish")

Local potatoes have skins that are safe to eat, unlike commercial, conventional potatoes which have some of the highest tested levels of added chemicals for "storage reasons." So don't eat skins from lesser grade spuds.

When the potatoes are freshly harvested (new), they are best gently simmered at low temperatures (skins left on) until barely soft, with a small amount of butter added late. Or gently simmer in lightly salted water, drain when just soft, and then chill to very minimally dress as a salad. Their flavors are so clean that heavy seasoning wastes the potatoes.

If using promptly, do not refrigerate, as cold temperatures lead to increased (and sometimes unwelcome) sugars. When boiling always start with cold, salted water.

BLUE

With deep blue skin and flesh that almost appears purple, here is another potato to brighten your table and your favorite potato salad. A favorite for making French fries or oven fries.

GREEN MOUNTAIN

This white potato is more oblong than round shaped. Like other high-starch potatoes, it's excellent for boiling and baking - great flavor! Deep eyes make this not so pretty - but the flavor makes up for it.

KATAHDIN

A low starch potato, traditional to Maine. Waxy white flesh and thin buff skin.

KENNEBEC
Kennebecs are superb boiled, mashed, fried, hashed or baked. Good jacket potato - smother it in sour cream, cheese, chives and bacon.

RED NORLAND
Smooth skin, white flesh, medium to large sized tubers. Excellent boiled and in salads. This potato has just enough starch that makes it good for frying as well as boiling for potato salad.

RED PONTIAC
Round tubers with red skin, medium-deep eyes and moist, crisp, white flesh. They are good for baking, salads and roasting.

YUKON GOLD
Attractive, smooth, thin yellow skin, and yellow flesh, it's versatile for most potato preparations – roasted or mashed. Their sweet flavor yields a rich mashed potato even without butter.

Pumpkins

To create your own "pumpkin pack" like purchased in cans at the supermarket: cut the pumpkin in half, and bake in a shallow dish with water, cut side down for an hour until soft. Scoop out seeds and set aside for another use. Purée the pulp in a food processor and freeze in portion controlled containers. For a moister pie, simmer peeled chunks until soft. The seeds can be de-pulped, rinsed and roasted with soy sauce, or olive oil and salt.

The seeds used for pepitas are a different variety, and these should not be used as a substitute.

JACK-O-LANTERN
Lovely to look at, lovely to carve, but have been bred more for Halloween than for cooking; often flavor-deficient.

NECK PUMPKIN
Also called the Pennsylvania Dutch Crookneck, these pumpkins look more like a butternut squash on steroids, often weighing as much as 15 pounds each. You can get enough "pumpkin pack" from each one to bake 6-8 pies, which is the best use for these. Rated by many as the best for pure pumpkin flavor and ease of use.

PIE PUMPKIN
Often ovoid in shape, typically more moist than neck or jack-o-lantern pumpkins. Excellent for cooking.

Radishes

Really nice sliced thinly in sandwiches of crusty bread, nice cheese, and/or roast beef, turkey, or ham. If they are too peppery for your taste, they can be roasted with butter and soy sauce for a refreshing spring or autumn side dish.

CHINA ROSE
Classic pungent winter radish, best sliced but not peeled; not at all mild. Very nice sliced thinly and smeared with brie, chèvre, or butter. Can also be chopped and added to cold salads of cucumbers, greens, tuna, beans, or egg. Tops can be cooked like turnip greens.

DAIKON
Daikon is an Asian variety: crisp, white, mild sweet radish. It's about 2 -3 inches in diameter and several inches long. Unlike other radishes, this variety can be peeled. Daikon and carrots can be mixed together for an easy, quick pickle: Season matchstick cut veggies with equal parts sugar and vinegar. Add salt to taste.

FRENCH BREAKFAST AND PINK BEAUTY
The most mild of radishes, fine any way you use the traditional red radish.

WATERMELON
An heirloom variety of the Asian winter radish, they are larger than a French breakfast and rounder than a daikon. They can be peeled, exposing the bright fuchsia center. Sliced raw, they add brilliant color to salads or crudités platters. They can also be cooked, but best with honey added to the simmering liquid.

WHITE ICICLE
Midway in pungency between China Rose and French Breakfast, with similar uses. Probably related to the daikons.

Raspberries

With just a touch of acidity, raspberries have a perfectly balanced sweetness that makes them ideal for desserts, savory dishes or just straight snacking. If puréeing to make a dessert sauce, be sure to strain out the seeds.

Rosemary

The pine-like scent of rosemary comes alive when grilled. The woody stems can act as kebab skewers for grilled vegetables. A few sprigs enhance roasted potatoes, chicken, steak or lamb. Sprinkled on fresh baked breads or infused in olive oil, rosemary is quite versatile. Like sage, a little rosemary can go a long way, so it is best to be judicious.

Rutabaga

Two possible varieties: one more elongate and more intense than turnips, the other round like a turnip and milder in flavor. Excellent raw or in soups, stews, purées, risotto, or roasted. Balance and complexity superior to that of turnips. We don't peel. Can be used for recipes that call for turnips but more of a performer when slow cooked.

Sage

Sage is a tricky herb – added fresh to a dish, a little (just a Tbs fresh chopped) goes a long way. But if you fry the leaves and sprinkle with a little salt, they entice like potato chips: deep fry the leaves in plain oil until just translucent. Strain with a slotted spoon and drain on a paper towel, and season them with salt. The leaves seem thinner and melt in your mouth.

Sage has many medicinal qualities, including: reduces bad breath, reduces perspiration, reduces the symptoms of menopause and premenstrual cramps, increases brain concentration, and reduces blood sugar in people with diabetes. Be cautioned, if you are pregnant, you should not consume sage in great quantity.

Squash Blossoms

Squash flowers are a favorite in France and Italy, but are served in the US more rarely. They can be scrambled with eggs, mixed into light risotto or pasta dishes, broiled at the last minute on top of mostly-cooked focaccia or white pizza, or stuffed and then deep-fried. Two excellent approaches for squash flowers are in the recipes section. Squash flowers are extraordinarily perishable, must be kept chilled at all times after harvest and must be used within three days.

Squash, Summer

Yellow squash tends to be sweeter and crunchier than the green zucchini. Yellow squash pairs well with traditional American summer flavors like corn and tomatoes. Zucchini blends well with Mediterranean flavors like tomatoes, olives and eggplants. Both varieties can be grilled or sautéed.

Smaller squash are more tender and can also be cut into sticks as a great addition to traditional crudités platters. Larger squash have a tough texture and are ideal for zucchini breads, puréed soups, ratatouille or caponata.

Some of the more traditional yellow summer squashes, especially from the South, can have tough skins even when picked young. Despite the tough skin, the flesh is sweeter and more tender. Simply peel the squash as you would a carrot or cucumber.

Squash, Winter

Winter squash are not squash grown during the winter. They are squash grown in the warm months and harvested in August or later; their thick skins let us store these for later use. Some can even keep until winter. Because of their shape, winter squash can be difficult to peel and handle raw. We recommend cooking them first and then scooping out the flesh. If you decide to cut them before cooking, it's easiest when they are at room temperature. These varieties of winter squash are particularly well suited for puréed preparations – served as a "mash," or as a base for creamy soups.

ACORN

Classic, New England winter squash for roasting or baking with maple syrup and butter. Its shape makes it ideal for stuffing.

BUTTERNUT

One of the longest-storing of all winter squash. Much appreciated in creamy autumn soups. It can be cubed and baked, or boiled and puréed.

SPAGHETTI

This is one of the few winter squash that merits special non-baked handling. Can be briefly microwaved or steamed and the strands "forked" out. Very versatile in salads, mixed in sautés, etcetera.

BUTTERCUP

A superb winter squash, with some of the finest flavor of all varieties. Slow, gentle cooking yields a sublime, custard-like texture and flavor.

BLUE HUBBARD

These tough-skinned winter squash with a golden yellow flesh can weigh as much as 15 pounds. Texturally, they tend to be dry and sometimes mealy, but the flavor is nutty and sweet, and extremely popular in New England. They are best roasted and puréed, in either a soup or pie.

Safely break open a Hubbard by placing it in a large plastic or paper bag and then dropping it on the ground.

Strawberries

Strawberries are the delicate jewel of spring. They are best eaten straight from the container to savor their sweet, juicy flavor. They are also a lovely addition to a spring salad, dressed simply with red wine vinegar, olive oil and fresh thyme.

Best washed by immersion: fill a large bowl or sink with cold water. Add the strawberries and swish them around a little. Let the dirt settle to the bottom, no more than 30 seconds, and then lift the strawberries out to drain in a colander. You will see the grit that simple rinsing under the faucet does not get rid of.

Sweet Potatoes

Fingerling sweets are starchier than big ones and are outstanding left skin-on, chunked, and then roasted with garlic. The really big sweet potatoes are the most easily peeled for subsequent steaming, grating, or pie-making, but are also the fastest to chunk for a quick roast. Very large sweet potatoes are unjustly scorned by novices, but old-time Southern cooks treasure the mammoths for ease of use. They also know that a slowly grown but big sweet potato is more flavorful than a typical conventionally grown, smaller sweet potato whose growth was rushed and babied with agricultural chemicals. Finally, the classic middle sizes are good for baking whole and for individual servings. Sweet potatoes should be washed once more and then stored in the pantry.

Recent studies have well documented that lowering the baking temperatures to 325°F or 340°F maximizes sweetness. If you want consistently really sweet, sweet potatoes, keep the baking temperatures low.

BEAUREGARD
Orange, creamy, not too sweet, and with very full and nuanced flavors. Our absolute favorite orange type.

COVINGTON
Orange as well but so sweet that it oozes sugary syrup while cooking!

WHITE HAMON
Beige to milk-white and with a nutty, nuanced suite of flavors. Absolute

best for frying but fine baked as well. Never boil, as this can turn the flesh grey-green.

JAPANESE PURPLE-SKIN WHITE FLESHED
A great white sweet potato. Has typical nuttiness and subtlety, but has unique chestnut-like flavor if slowly baked past the softened stage.

O'HENRY
Smooth-skinned and mild; is most like Irish potatoes in texture and flavor. Can be creamy and very sweet under ideal growing conditions.

Tarragon
The soft leaves have a flavor reminiscent of licorice and basil. It enhances many dishes – tomatoes, asparagus, beef and salmon.

Thyme
A great all-purpose herb. A few sprigs add zest to sautéed mushrooms, stewed meats, chicken soup, or roasted potatoes.

Tomatillos
These are the husk tomatoes that so confuse many non-Mexican cooks. The sticky papery husk obscures a potential gem and must be removed. Store-bought tomatillos are nearly always picked very under ripe and are usually dark green and bitter. In contrast, local farmers can let them fully ripen on the vine, where they sweeten wonderfully, develop nearly apple- or melon-like flavors, and turn a very pale green-yellow or even purple. Tomatillos can be grilled or roasted or turned into a green chile salsa, but properly ripened ones are so good that we prefer raw uses.

After de-husking, slice raw into salads, use for dipping, or top slices with a nice Cheddar, Gouda, chèvre, or fresh mozzarella. Less ripe ones can be baked with olive oil and salt to become the vital base for salsa verde.

Tomatoes
All tomatoes should be taken out of their packaging once you get them home. Larger tomatoes are best stored on their shoulders (where the stem was attached), separated from each other on a counter until fully ripe. Windowsills are used if you want to speed ripening. Once ripe, tomatoes that cannot be eaten within 12-24 hours should be refrigerated before they rot. The transition from gloriously ripe to beginning to turn (the wrong way) is fastest in August, September, or when the toms have been harvested

right after intense summer heat or violent rains. Treat cherry toms the same, though these cannot easily be stored on their shoulders.

We use two iron-clad rules for tomatoes: 1) the ripening enzymes inside each tomato are killed at 53° F by refrigeration, so chilling an under ripe tomato dooms you to poor flavors; and 2) a ripe but refrigerated tomato is much better than a tomato that slowly rots at room temp because we do not get around to eating it fast enough.

Cherry tomatoes are superbly convenient fast snacks for kids and adults, make lovely salsas and salads, and are usually more intensely flavorful than bigger tomatoes..

Tomatoes fall into four basic categories: plums, cherries, currants and larger slicers (the beefsteak types, weighing between 3 ounces and two pounds). The plums are generally the least flavorful, less juicy and best for cooking: they won't water down your sauces. Cherries and currants are best for snacking, but together with the beefsteak-types, can be used for cooking. Simply drain and reserve the extra juice (see stewed tomato recipe).

Heirlooms vary widely in color and ugly form, but have incredible flavor. Some are sweeter, others more acidic. Typically they are more juicy. As such, when cooked, they require long simmer times to reduce the liquid, and also to concentrate the flavors.

There are thousands of varieties. Here are some of the more popular ones we've seen available.

BOLSENO
They have green shoulders even when ripe. This Italian variety is slightly acidic, so vinegar is not necessary when making a salad.

BRANDYWINE
Most suitable for regions with cool summer nights, Brandywine is difficult to grow, but produces an amazing tomato. Only moderately acidic with superb depth of flavors and an almost buttery texture.

CELEBRITY
A hybrid tomato that produces deep red, medium to large fruit. Full flavored with a nice balance of sweetness and acidity. It's a great slicing tomato for sandwiches.

CHEROKEE PURPLE
A really ugly tomato, with green shoulders even when ripe, frequent cracking and purple-red-auburn mottled skin and flesh. But what flavor! Full, deep taste, with enough acidity to make you take notice. Very juicy as well. A really fine, bold heirloom; grown under the right conditions, among the most intense.

CHERRY AND GRAPE TOMATOES
Superbly convenient fast snacks for kids and adults! For salads and salsas, they are halved with a serrated knife.

HOMESTEAD AND RUTGERS
These large red beefsteak-types are classic American tomatoes, with lots of juice, moderate acidity, and good sweetness. Very good, though juicy, for sandwiches. Not as fully flavored or aggressive as many others, but very popular.

MORETON
The classic "Jersey" tomato, outstanding flavor, large and meaty.

MOUNTAIN JUBILEE
A gold beefsteak heirloom with superb balance of flavors, low to moderate acidity, low juice, and buttery texture.

ORANGE BLOSSOM
A yellowish/orange tomato with a mild flavor and low acidity.

PINK GIRL
A hybrid tomato, large and juicy. These tomatoes are slightly sweet with a smooth skin.

PLUM TOMATOES
Lower water content (i.e., less juicy), makes them ideal for sauces and grilling. They typically have less flavor than cherries or heirlooms. The intensely flavored and juicy heirlooms can easily make too soupy a sauce: hence the plums. Frequently grown plum varieties are Roma, Amish Paste, San Marzano and Speckled Roman.

PRUDEN'S PURPLE

Really complex flavors, excellent texture, and only moderate acidity make this a worthy competitor to the venerable heirloom Brandywine. Pruden's is a bright pink to mottled purple, often large, and nearly as funny looking as Cherokee Purple.

RED ZEBRA

A small, red tomato with orange stripes. They have excellent flavor, though rather acidic, making them a great compliment to grilled cheese sandwiches or caprese salads.

ROSE

An heirloom tomato with flavor similar to Brandywine. It is a large, pink beefsteak.

STRIPED GERMAN

A beautiful juicy tomato with red and yellow stripes. It has sweet, complex flavors with a smooth texture.

SUNBRITE

Firm, meaty tomato, less sweet than other varieties. When dressing these tomatoes, use less vinegar than the typical ratio of 3:1, oil: vinegar.

SUNGOLD

A hybrid cherry tomato that revitalized the commercial cherry tomato world with its superb, intense flavor.

SUN SUGAR

Yellow cherry tomato.

SUNSTART

Large firm fruit produce early in the season.

SWEET ONE HUNDRED

A red cherry tomato with flavors often as intense as Sungold.

SWEET TANGERINE

Medium sized fruit with a tangerine color, they ripen earlier than other varieties. They are very sweet and flavorful – perfect for salads.

SWEETHEARTS

A very sweet cherry tomato.

YELLOW AND RED BRANDYMASTER
Firm and juicy tomatoes, with rich tomato flavor.

Turnips

Tender and outstanding roasted, braised, or simmered. Very nice raw, sliced
1/16"– 1/8" thin, then dipped into soy sauce or a vegetable dip. Peeling
optional. Tops (greens) may be washed once more and sautéed or braised as
per any of the chard recipes. Both roots and tops are very high in calcium
and potassium.

COLETTO VIOLA
An absolutely perfect heirloom turnip for simmering and then finishing
with butter. Long and slender, violet and white.

HAKUREI
Snow white and perfectly round, they are sweet and slightly earthy, crisp
and juicy. They are wonderful raw, or lightly cooked.

PURPLE TOP
The traditional turnip in much of the US; it can be boring when grown for
supermarkets, but its crisp texture and gentle flavors really shine when cold
grown.

SCARLET QUEEN
They look like a radish, but have a stem similar to a beet. They have more
kick than the other varieties. They can be eaten raw or cooked.

TOKYO
Slightly spicy when raw, they are buttery sweet when cooked.

Watermelon

In the best of summers –hot and tending toward drought—watermelons
are at their finest. In cool wet summers they are not as sweet or perfect but
they are still better than store-bought. Good watermelons are not just for
eating as cut fruit. They are also excellent (after de-seeding) in daiquiris
or as the base for a sorbet. For the latter, blend watermelon meat to make
3 cups. Add 3 Tbs corn syrup or no sugar at all, the juice of 1 lime, and
(optionally) 1 Tbs vodka. Put through an ice cream machine; re-freeze if
necessary. Superb, healthy and refreshing!

CHAPTER 3: Storing Your Produce for Optimal Freshness

Most fruits and vegetables can be grouped into simplifying categories that really help busy home cooks and chefs:

Produce that wants to be kept as cold as possible without freezing and preferably in a lidded container like a large Tupperware. Examples are most leafy greens, ripe berries, wild mushrooms, cucumbers, and radishes.

Produce that hates any refrigeration and wants a cool (or room temperature) pantry, basement, or kitchen. Examples are sweet potatoes and winter squash.

Produce that wants the warmer part of the fridge but suffers if too cold. Includes basil, sorrel, and a few others.

Produce that likes refrigeration but can briefly be kept on the counter. Examples are watermelon and carrots.

Fruits that need ripening, but once ripe must be eaten soon or refrigerated. This group is the most complex and takes the most care. Refrigeration in these fruits will irreparably destroy the ripening enzymes within the fruits, thus dooming the foods to be under ripe and boring shadows of what they could have become. Examples include peaches and nectarines, but premature cooling of commercial tomatoes has made more Americans dissatisfied with mass-marketed tomatoes than with any other crop. Whenever possible, fruits in this category should be placed on a counter, slightly separated from each other, and not on their bellies but rather on their shoulders. The shoulders, most obvious with big tomatoes, are the part that surrounds where the stem was (or is). Once ripened at room temperature, fruits in this group are at the peak of flavor. At this

35

point they must be eaten very soon or refrigerated, as rotting will begin within 12 to 24 hours. A refrigerated ripe tomato or nectarine or avocado will keep for a few days and is much better than one that festers on the counter until thrown out. To maximize flavors, bring refrigerated ripe fruits back to room temperature before eating.

Storage areas also have subtle temperature differences that can also help you keep foods best:

The coldest areas of the fridge are usually the bottom, back, and crisper drawers; the door shelves are generally the warmest (e.g. better for basil)

Basements are usually cooler than pantries or closets. If dry, they are excellent for winter squashes and sweet potatoes.

Windowsills ripen tomatoes much faster than counter tops.

CANNING TOMATOES

Canning foods safely protects them from rot or off-flavors for 1 to 3 years. Canning used to be how many American families survived through winter before the advent of freezers and cheap (and more boringly flavored) commercial foods. It is still a superb technique to learn and use as part of the repertoire of accomplished cooks. The approach below use tomatoes as an example, but also works well with jellies, jams, and other vegetables packed in an acidic liquid.

The one thing to remember when canning tomatoes (or any other acidic foods) is that you need to boil everything. Boil the jars, boil the tomatoes and boil the tomatoes in the jar. The first two boils are necessary to sterilize the jars and the tomatoes, the third boil is to create a vacuum seal in the jar. This technique also works well for sauces and jams. For more tips on canning, refer to The Joy of Cooking *by Rombauer and Becker.*

So to be clear, the process goes like this:

1. Purchase canning jars. We prefer the wide mouth because they are easier to fill. Consider buying a variety of sizes. Even if you are only canning one kind of sauce, the variety will enable you to maximize your tomatoes – if a recipe calls for a small amount of tomato, you open a small jar, instead of opening a large jar that may not be completely used. Also, buy a pair of "canning tongs". These tongs are specially designed to lift the jars out of the water.

2. Wash the jars. Put the lids and bands in one pot and the jars in another pot. The pot for the jars should be deep enough that the top of the jars can be covered by at least one inch of water.

3. Cover the jars completely with water and bring them to a boil. Continue boiling them for 10 minutes.

4. Cover the lids completely with water and put them on the stove. Bring to a boil, and turn off the heat. Let them sit in the water until you're ready to use them.

5. Meanwhile, wash and coarsely chop tomatoes. Put them in a stainless steel (non-aluminum) pot. Bring the tomatoes to a boil, and continue cooking them for at least 10 minutes. Even if you smoked the tomatoes, you still need to boil them.

6. Remove the jars from the water, draining the water out. Fill each jar with tomatoes, be sure to leave at least a ½-inch air-gap at the top. With a clean towel, wipe the lip of each jar clean.

7. Drain the water from the lids and cover each jar. Screw on the metal band, but not too tightly.

8. Return the jars to the boiling water and let boil for 10 minutes. Remove from the water and let stand for 20 minutes. Remove the band and test the seal of the lids – if it comes off easily, then the seal did not work and you must repeat the process. If the lid is tight, then you are all set! Otherwise, remove lid, and wipe rim of jar clean with a sterilized towel. Reseal jar with lid and band, and return to pot of boiling water for 5 minutes more.

MORE DETAILED STORAGE GUIDE

We have prepared this list to help you best enjoy your seasonal produce, and how to time which foods to eat first when you pick up your CSA subscription or arrive home from the farmers' market.

We have used our decades of experience as restaurant chefs to advise you on how to best store your foods. While there are numerous beliefs on correct storage, the approaches that follow have been tested on many thousands of cases of wholesale produce.

Enjoy your great local fruits and vegetables, and store them well!

APPLES Shelf Life: 5-26 weeks
Coldest part of the fridge. Soften after some months, but fine for cooking after that.

BASIL, ALL TYPES Shelf Life: 2-5 days
Cut stems in vase with water on counter top is best, or in the warmest part of the refrigerator. Excessive cold blackens the leaves.

LONG TERM STORAGE
Wash and dry leaves. Purée in a food processor with about 1 Tbs olive oil for every 1 cup of leaves. Spoon into ice cube trays and freeze. When frozen solid, cubes can be transferred to a Ziploc bag.

BEETS Shelf Life: roots: 5 weeks; greens: 5 days
Best in fridge, but OK in basement. Separate greens - must be refrigerated. Wash greens just before cooking.

BLACKBERRIES Shelf Life: 3 - 5 days
Must be refrigerated: coldest part of fridge. If storing in a plastic container, pack loosely. It's also okay to store in an open container. Wash right before eating/using. Excess undrained water leads to fungal growth.

BLUEBERRIES Shelf Life: 1 - 2 weeks
Must be refrigerated: coldest part of fridge. Wash only before eating/using. Excess water leads to fungal growth.

LONG TERM STORAGE
Line a cookie sheet with parchment or wax paper. Lay blueberries in a single layer and freeze overnight. Once frozen, they can be transferred to a Ziploc bag.

BROCCOLI Shelf Life: 1 - 2 weeks
Refrigerate in coldest part of fridge. Best with a moist towel on top to keep crisp.

BRUSSELS SPROUTS Shelf Life: Keeps 3-4 weeks
Coldest part of the fridge.

CABBAGE - GREEN Shelf Life: Refrigerated up to 4 months
Best anywhere in the fridge. Can be stored in a very cold basement if needed, but not ideal.

CABBAGE - CHINESE Shelf Life: 5-21 days
Any part of fridge.

CARROTS Shelf Life: 3 months, properly stored
Coldest part of the fridge. Best to store dry (in a bag). If they are too wet they will start to sprout or rot. Out of the bag they begin to go flaccid. Cellar only with great care.

CAULIFLOWER Shelf Life: 1 - 2 weeks
Refrigerate in coldest part of fridge.

CELERIAC Shelf Life: Up to 3 months
Fridge is best, but pantry or cellar works okay too.

CELERY Shelf Life: 1 - 3 weeks
Coldest part of fridge. Leaves like to be dry in a bag. Stems like to be loose in a bag.

CILANTRO Shelf Life: 3 - 14 days
Washed, drained and then refrigerated. In a sealed Tupperware, with a paper towel or cloth underneath to help regulate the moisture.

CORN (POPPING) Shelf Life: 9 months
Sealed jar in pantry is best. Pops best if used within 9 months of harvest.

CORN (SWEET) Shelf Life: Best to eat immediately, but will retain sweetness up to 4 days
Coldest part of the fridge. Typically loses sweetness during storage.

LONG TERM STORAGE
Cut kernels off the cob. Store in a Ziploc bag in the freezer for up to 6 months.

CUCUMBERS Shelf Life: 3-10 days
Refrigerate.

LONG TERM STORAGE
See Recipes for pickling suggestions.

DILL Shelf Life: 3 - 14 days
Washed, drained and then refrigerated. In a sealed Tupperware, with a paper towel or cloth underneath to help regulate the moisture.

LONG TERM STORAGE
Wash and thoroughly dry. Put in a Ziploc bag and freeze. No need to defrost before using.

EDAMAME (SOY BEANS) Shelf Life: 7 days
Store refrigerated, unwashed.

EGGPLANT Shelf Life: 7-10 days upon refrigeration
On counter until ripe and soft (and a little wrinkly) -- this is mildest and most tender. When ripe put in fridge.

FENNEL BULBS Shelf Life: 1 - 3 weeks
Coldest part of fridge. Leaves like to be dry in a bag. Stems like to be loose in a bag.

FIGS Shelf Life: Best eaten immediately
Even in the fridge, they will only keep for two days before starting to mold.

GARLIC Shelf Life: Best flavor when eaten within 6 weeks, but can keep up to 4 months
Pantry.

GREEN BEANS/STRING BEANS Shelf Life: 3- 10 days
Refrigerator - loose and dry.

GREENS
All greens should be washed and drained before storing in the refrigerator. Longest shelf life is had by placing greens on top of a paper towel or clean cloth inside of a lidded Tupperware container. Whole heads store longer and better than cut leaves.

Arugula Shelf Life: 3 - 14 days
Bok Choy Shelf Life: 1 - 3 weeks
Collards Shelf Life: 3 - 14 days
Cress Shelf Life: 3 - 7 days
Endive (Belgian) Shelf Life: 1 - 8 weeks
Frisee Shelf Life: 5 - 14 days
Kale Shelf Life: 3 - 14 days
Lettuce Shelf Life: 3 - 7 days
Mesclun Shelf Life: 2 - 5 days
Mizuna Shelf Life: 7 - 10 days
Mustard Greens Shelf Life: 3 - 10 days
Pak Choi Shelf Life: 3-21 days
Pea Tendrils Shelf Life: 3 - 5 days
Radicchio Shelf Life: 1 - 3 weeks
Sorrel Shelf Life: 1 -7 days
Spinach Shelf Life: 2 - 5 days
Swiss Chard Shelf Life: 3-14 days
Tat Soi Shelf Life: 1 - 3 weeks

HORSERADISH Shelf Life: Many months
Coldest part of fridge.

JERUSALEM ARTICHOKES Shelf Life: Many months
Coldest part of fridge, loose and dry in paper or plastic bag.

KOHLRABI Shelf Life: 1 - 6 weeks
Coldest part of fridge, loose and dry in plastic bag.

LEEKS Shelf Life: 5 - 30 days
Coldest part of fridge, loose and dry in plastic bag.

MELONS (CANTALOUPE) Shelf Life: Up to 2 weeks (after ripe) in fridge
On counter until ripe. Refrigerating will slow or stop the ripening if necessary. Cantaloupe smells perfumed and ripe from the stem end when perfect; the flesh will be meltingly soft when fully ripe. At this point, eat within 24 hours or refrigerate.

MELONS (HONEYDEW) Shelf Life: Up to 5 weeks in the fridge
Treat as per watermelon. Very hard to determine ripeness at purchase or thereafter.

MINT Shelf Life: 2-5 days
Cut stems in vase with water on counter top is best, or in the warmest part of the refrigerator. Excessive cold blackens the leaves.

LONG TERM STORAGE
Wash and thoroughly dry. Put in a Ziploc bag and freeze. No need to defrost before using.

MUSHROOMS, WILD Shelf Life: 1–5 days
Immediately refrigerate when you return home from the market. Best stored in a paper bag or in Tupperware with a paper towel. Do not store in a plastic bag. Wash immediately before using. Porcinis and honeys are ideally used within 12 hours. Morels, oysters, maitake and shiitake can last up to 2-4 weeks in the 'fridge. Once cooked, they freeze superbly.

NECTARINES Shelf Life: Once ripened and refrigerated: 3 - 5 days
On counter top, loose and separated on platter, until just soft. Fruit should sit on its shoulders. Once ripe, eat within 12 hours or refrigerate.

OKRA Shelf Life: 3-7 days
Refrigerated, dry and loose in bag. Wash only immediately before using.

ONIONS (DRY SKIN) Shelf Life: 2 - 20 weeks
Pantry or basement.

ONIONS (GREEN AND SPRING) Shelf Life: 3-14 days
Must be refrigerated.

OREGANO Shelf Life: 2 - 5 days
Do not wash! Store loose in a bag in the warmest part of refrigerator. Best if used quickly.

PARSLEY Shelf Life: 4 - 21 days
Washed, drained and then refrigerated. In a sealed Tupperware, with a paper towel or cloth underneath to help regulate the moisture.

LONG TERM STORAGE
Wash and thoroughly dry. Put in a Ziploc bag and freeze. No need to defrost before using.

PARSNIPS Shelf Life: 3 months
Coldest part of the fridge. Best to store dry (in a bag). If they are too wet they will start to sprout or rot. Out of the bag they begin to go flaccid. Cellar only with great care.

PEACHES Shelf Life: Once ripened and refrigerated: 3 - 5 days
On counter top, loose and separated on platter, until just soft. Fruit should sit on its shoulders. Once ripe, eat within 12 hours or refrigerate.

PEAS (ENGLISH) Shelf Life: 1 - 3 weeks, but sweetest eaten within 1-4 days after harvest
Refrigerator, keep in the bag. Shell as soon as pods soften.

PEAS (SNOW, SUGAR SNAP) Shelf Life: 3 - 14 days
Coldest part of fridge.

PEPPERS (GREEN - SWEET) Shelf Life: 1 - 5 weeks
Refrigerate, loose and dry.

PEPPERS (HOT) Shelf Life: 1 - 5 weeks
Refrigerate, loose and dry.

LONG TERM STORAGE
Cut into rings, then pack in vinegar or freeze.

PEPPERS (RED - SWEET) Shelf Life: 3 - 21 days
Refrigerate, loose and dry.

LONG TERM STORAGE
Place peppers over a gas burner (or under a broiler) until the skin is blackened on all sides. Put peppers in a bowl, cover with plastic wrap and let steam for 10 minutes. When peppers are cool, peel or rub away blackened skin. Cut in half; remove and discard the stem and seeds. Toss with olive oil. Freeze in 1 cup containers.

PLUMS Shelf Life: Once ripened and refrigerated: 3 - 5 days.
On counter top, loose and separated on platter, until just soft. Once ripe, eat within 12 hours or refrigerate.

POTATOES ("IRISH", BUT ACTUALLY FROM THE ANDES) Shelf Life: Up to 4 months in fridge, 6 months maximum in cool cellar or pantry
Pantry, cellar or warmest part of the fridge. Very cold temperatures lead to increased sugar/sweetness; nice for some people, unexpected for others. New potatoes, on the other hand, must be refrigerated.

PUMPKINS Shelf Life: 3 - 8 weeks
In a cool basement (55 -65°F) or pantry. Hate refrigeration.

RADISHES Shelf Life: 1 - 5 weeks
Washed, drained and then refrigerated, in a Tupperware with a paper towel or cloth underneath to help regulate the moisture.

RASPBERRIES Shelf Life: 1-3 days
Must be refrigerated in coldest part of fridge. If storing in a plastic container, pack loosely. Okay to store in an open container. Wash only before eating/using: excessive or premature washing leads to fungal growth.

ROSEMARY Shelf Life: 1 - 2 weeks
Do not wash! Store dried, loose in a bag in any part of refrigerator.

RUTABAGA Shelf Life: 2 - 7 weeks
Loose and dry in any part of the refrigerator.

SAGE Shelf Life: 2 - 5 days
Do not wash! Store loose in a bag in the warmest part of refrigerator. Best if used immediately.

SQUASH BLOSSOMS Shelf Life: 1-3 days
Refrigerate ASAP! Store in a lidded Tupperware with a moist paper towel in the bottom.

LONG TERM STORAGE
May be stuffed, dredged, and then frozen (see recipes).

SQUASH, SUMMER (ALL) Shelf Life: 3-10 days
Refrigerate.

SQUASH, WINTER (ACORN, BUTTERCUP, DELICATA, HUBBARD, KABOCHA)
Shelf Life: 1 – 5 months, depending on variety and growing conditions
In a cool basement, pantry or counter top (55 -65°F). Hate refrigeration.

SQUASH, WINTER (BUTTERNUT, SPAGHETTI) Shelf Life: 3 weeks - 6 months, depending on variety and growing conditions
In a cool basement, pantry or counter top (55 -65°F). Hate refrigeration.

STRAWBERRIES Shelf Life: 1-3 days
Must be refrigerated in coldest part of fridge. If storing in a plastic container, pack loosely. Best to store in an open container. Wash only before eating/using: excessive or premature washing leads to fungal growth.

LONG TERM STORAGE
Wash and stem berries. Put in a pot with 1/4 cup of water and 1-2 Tbs of sugar for every cup of berries. Simmer over medium heat until soft. Purée and freeze.

SWEET POTATOES Shelf Life: 5 weeks - 8 months, depending on variety and previous handling
Hate refrigeration: NEVER in fridge. Basement or Pantry. Ideally at 55 - 65°F, but tolerates up to 80°F or higher.

TARRAGON Shelf Life: 4 - 7 days
Dry, loose in a plastic bag in the coldest part of the refrigerator. Wash just before using. You can also pack it in vinegar or white wine upon receipt -- it will keep indefinitely this way.

THYME Shelf Life: 1 - 2 weeks
Do not wash! Store loose in a bag in any part of refrigerator.

TOMATILLOS Shelf Life: 10 – 14 days in refrigerator
Keep on counter top until ripe (pale yellow/green inner skin and softening of fruit).

TOMATOES, BIG SLICING Shelf Life: Once ripened and refrigerated: 3 - 5 days
Counter top, loose and separated on platter, until just soft. On shoulders as per peaches and nectarines.

LONG TERM STORAGE
See canning directions. Alternatively, make sauce or stewed tomatoes (see detailed recipes) and freeze.

TOMATOES, CHERRY Shelf Life: in refrigerator: 7 - 10 days
Assuming they arrive ripe, eat within 12 hours or refrigerate. If under-ripe, store in open container on counter until fully ripe.

LONG TERM STORAGE
See canning directions. Alternatively, make sauce or stewed tomatoes (see detailed recipes) and freeze.

TOMATOES, PLUMS Shelf Life: in refrigerator: up to 10 days
Store loose on counter, separated from each other, until ripe. Use or refrigerate within 24 hours.

LONG TERM STORAGE
See canning directions. Alternatively, make sauce or stewed tomatoes (see detailed recipes) and freeze.

TURNIPS Shelf Life: 2 - 7 weeks
Loose and dry in any part of the refrigerator.

WATERMELON Shelf Life: 3 - 5 weeks
Counter storage will not much help ripening, but much more tolerant of pantry, fridge or basement storage than other melons.

CHAPTER 4: Key Techniques and Definitions of Terms

WASHING LEAFY GREENS: Most vegetables can be washed under cool (not cold) running water. The exception to this is the leafy greens. Nothing ruins a meal more than biting into a mouthful of sandy, gritty greens.

To properly wash greens and rid them of dirt: fill a large bowl or sink with cool water. Put the greens in the water and gently swoosh them around. Let them sit for a minute to let the dirt settle to the bottom. Lift the greens out of the water and place them in a colander to let the water drain. Do not pour the greens with the water into the colander as the grit that has settled to the bottom will reintroduce itself into the leaves. For really gritty greens, repeat this process with clean water. This technique is also recommended for parsley, cilantro, wild mushrooms and berries.

BAKING AND ROASTING are often used for the vegetables of late summer, most especially the "winter" squash (grown during the summer, but suitable for storage and use during the colder months) and sweet potatoes. Farm-fresh eggs also perform superbly in baking. They are so fresh relative to store-bought that cakes and soufflés made with them are much more airy, as is the fried-then-baked Italian omelet, the frittata.

Roasting is a subset of baking. In this simplest of cookbooks, roasting usually means adding seasoning and olive oil, baking between 340°F and 425°F until nearly soft, then adding (if desired) chopped onion, garlic, and herbs.

TO BLANCH is to briefly (10-90 seconds) steam or boil, usually followed by shocking in an ice bath. Used more with the winter cooking greens.

BOILING is unjustifiably looked down upon as a "common" cooking

45

technique. Boiling can make tough greens or old stewing chickens more tender than can anything except a pressure cooker. Boiling can also dispel or dilute the occasionally bitter flavors of some vegetables. We always add about 1 tsp salt per quart of water to preserve both the color and some of the nutrients that can be lost by non-careful boiling. Be sure, too, that the water is fully boiling (medium and small bubbles coming up from the pot's bottom) or rolling more vigorously. Simmering is a more gentle boil, with only small bubbles coming up. Simmering is the main technique for many a great tomato sauce.

TO BRAISE is to cook under low to moderate heat, with plenty of water, broth, beer, or wine, until soft. Excellent for bigger summer squash, for the winter squash, for non-bitter, cold-season greens, for some meats, and for "comfort food" approaches. Cooking times vary from only 20 or 30 seconds (the most tender greens) to as long as 2 hours (some meats).

GRILLING means cooking over an open flame and usually on top of a grate. We grill many summer vegetables: summer squash, plum tomatoes, skewered cherry tomatoes, tomatillos, sweet peppers, sweet potato slices, and even par-boiled potatoes. Even at its simplest, good grilling of vegetables should involve brushing them sparingly with vegetable oil and seasoning with salt and pepper. More complex marinades can include soy sauce, wine, minced onion and garlic, herbs, ginger, etc.

DEEP FRYING adds textural contrast and interest to many vegetables, but given that it adds many calories to a recipe, we recommend saving this technique for special occasions. To properly deep fry, you will need a heavy-bottom 3-quart pot and plenty of plain oil. If you have a "fry daddy," even better. A slotted spoon or Chinese wire-mesh spoon is the best tool for fetching food out of the oil. Always drain on a paper towel or newspaper to absorb excess grease.

The secret to non-greasy deep-fried foods is making sure the oil is properly heated and not overcrowded. A candy thermometer is the best tool to ensure the oil is properly heated. In a pinch, a wooden spoon acts as a good gauge: put the spoon in the oil – when bubbles vigorously form around the spoon, the oil is hot. By not adding too much food to the oil at one time, the oil maintains its temperature. Heat the oil over a medium high heat. When the oil reaches the proper temperature, 350°F to 375°F, turn the heat down to medium and monitor to make sure the temperature stays within that range.

Nearly all fried foods signal they are done not by color, but by sound. Food that has just been put in the oil crackles very loudly from all the moisture. Once the food floats, it will turn down the volume somewhat, but there's an abrupt shift into pretty quiet just when it hits the perfect point.

OIL here means oil from vegetables, seeds, or nuts. We advocate using oils to protect broiling, grilling, or roasting foods from drying out, to better conduct heat in the context of grilling, and in the more traditional sense to prevent foods in a skillet from sticking. In the Italianate approach we prefer, we rarely fry or sauté in pure butter (a fat, not an oil), but rather sparingly use butter added late to a sauté process or even as a final seasoning.

We recommend stocking 3 oils: extra-virgin olive oil; any relatively neutral oil like peanut, corn, or canola; and dark sesame oil such as Kadoya. Extra-virgin olive oil is strongly perfumed, outstanding in salads or roasted vegetables, but easily burned and costly for sauté. Sesame oil acts in much the same way but is of Asian origin. We therefore often blend either of the two strongly-flavored oils above with the intentionally neutral corn, peanut, or canola oil. The neutral oils elevate the temperatures at which the olive or sesame oils alone would burn, as well as decreasing cost and toning down the overwhelming flavors of the premium oils. A neutral oil such as canola or peanut is ideal for deep-frying.

POACHING is a most temperature-sensitive, gentle technique. It means barely cooking greens, eggs, or most famously fish in water or broth that is just below 212°F and that is rigorously guarded against that boiling point. Poaching respects tender foods better than any other cooking approach, though with chewier or tougher foods boiling remains a better choice. Poaching or blanching large whole tomatoes let us then shock them with ice water, peel the skins, and have skin-free tomato meats.

TO SHOCK is an essential step that follows boiling or steaming of many foods, from tomatoes, greens, and other vegetables to eggs and even shrimp. Shocking stops the cooking process precisely when you want by immediately plunging the really hot food into an ice water bath (recall that foods continue to cook from the time they are taken from the stove until the time they cool to room temperature). They are then drained promptly.

47

This keeps the lovely bright green of asparagus, beans, and leafy vegetables, as well as keeping textures crisp rather than becoming mushy. Nearly all vegetables and plain shrimp served in many restaurants are blanched and shocked, later seasoned, and possibly re-heated. Shocking gives busy cooks insurance against overcooking. Ice water is our friend.

STEAMING is one of the hottest and fastest ways to cook, but adds little flavor (in contrast with sautéing or grilling). Western steamers are good, but a wok and stackable bamboo steamers, available in good Asian markets, remain our favorite. Be sure to start with at least ¾-inch of water for fast steaming and at least 3 cups of water for long steaming. Put your food in the steamer after it has fully heated up and is vigorously steaming.

ON POTS AND PANS: We urge you to consider pruning your kitchens of potentially hazardous cookware. Cookware coated with Teflon or other synthetics always slowly and imperceptibly lose their finish, and molecules of Teflon are now being routinely discovered in alarming amounts in human tissues and in the environment. Enameled pots (e.g. Le Creuset) are outstanding, but only if the enamel finish is entirely intact. Less strident cautions are apt for solid aluminum pots. Aluminum appears to be OK except for acidic cooking (like tomato sauce) but unambiguous data on the health effects of aluminum aren't yet present.

So what pans to use? Cast iron makes the absolute best for skillets and woks, and cultures that still favor cast iron have lower incidences of anemia (any iron that leaches out into your food acts as a vital nutrient; not so with aluminum or Teflon). The only drawbacks are that iron pans weigh more and react with acidic foods. For deep frying and large volumes of stew we use cast iron Dutch ovens, though the weight necessitates lifting these with two hands when full.

And for boiling water, as well as all sizes of saucepans, high-quality, thick-bottomed stainless steel is super.

Finally, having both a blender and a food processor will make cooking much easier. We loathe any surplus of kitchen gadgets but find these indispensable. It should also be noted that a blender makes a poor substitute for a food processor, and a food processor rarely purées as smoothly as a blender – hence the need for both.

CHAPTER 5: The Recipes

The recipes in this book range from super-simple with just a few ingredients to more complex, multi-component dishes. There are soups, salads, side dishes, entrees and desserts. All give you new and interesting ways to enjoy your fresh produce.

Unlike many cookbooks, we organized the savory recipes alphabetically by primary ingredient, from apples to watermelon (zucchini is in the squash section). In the back, we separated out the recipes for sauces, dressings and vinaigrettes; the sweeter dishes and a few beverages are at the end.

We've each cooked professionally for over 15 years. Like many chefs, we've tired of our own cooking, so when we get together we love eating each other's creations. But we have distinct personalities… which perhaps you will pick up on. Most notably, Julia seasons all her recipes with salt, pepper and lemon juice, whereas Brett is more likely to use beer or wine for a final flourish.

The other big distinction, perhaps less obvious, is Brett's substantially larger appetite than Julia's – no doubt from hours working in the fields planting, harvesting and working the land. By Julia's standards, Brett's recipes could feed a family of four for a week. And Brett could easily make a single meal out of recipe Julia thinks would feed 6.

The recipes generally yield four to six servings. The number of servings you get will depend on who you're serving and what you're serving with the dish.

APPLE AND HAZELNUT HASH

This is a perfect autumnal accompaniment to roast chicken or pork.

2 Tbs canola oil
½ bunch of sage, stems removed
¼ cup hazelnuts, coarsely chopped
2 cloves garlic, sliced
1 red onion, thinly sliced

3 apples (3 different kinds is ideal), cored and sliced (skin left on)
1 tsp fresh thyme
salt and pepper to taste

1. In a large sauté pan, heat oil over a high flame. Add the sage leaves (whole) and the hazelnuts. When the hazelnuts begin to brown, add the garlic slices. When the garlic slices begin to brown, remove from heat. Scoop out "crispies" with a slotted spoon and drain on a paper towel. Leave remaining oil in the pan. Season "crispies" with salt and pepper.

2. Return pan to heat, add onions. When the onions begin to turn translucent, add apples. Let apples sit for a few minutes, without stirring, so that they may brown. Season with salt, pepper and thyme.

3. Right before serving, mix apples with "crispies".

GREEN BEANS WITH CHILIES AND LIME

This dish is inspired by the small cafés in Bali. Snow peas or snap peas would also work well in this dish, but reduce the cooking time drastically.

1 Tbs oil

2 Tbs chopped garlic

1 ½-inch ginger, chopped

2 chili peppers, de-seeded and diced (more or less to taste)

½ pound green beans, snipped

½ head of shredded green cabbage

½ tsp sugar

1 lime, zested (or 3 lime leaves, finely chopped)

salt, pepper and lime juice to taste

1 cup bean sprouts

2 Tbs fried shallots*

1. Heat a large skillet, and add oil. Add garlic, ginger and chilies and cook until the mixture becomes aromatic, about 2 minutes.

2. Add green beans and cabbage and sauté, stirring frequently, until green beans are bright green. If the pan seems dry, add ¼ cup of water. If using sugar snap or snow peas, cook the cabbage first for 5 minutes before adding the peas.

3. Add sugar, lime zest and adjust seasoning to taste with salt, pepper and lime juice.

4. Toss green beans with bean sprouts and fried shallots.

*Fried shallots can be purchased at Asian supermarkets. Or you can make your own by frying thin slices of peeled shallots in plenty of canola oil over medium heat for 12 - 15 minutes, or until golden brown. Drain on a paper towel. Oil can be reserved for other cooking uses.

GREEN BEANS WITH SESAME DRESSING

This dressing would also be delicious with snow or snap peas.

8 Tbs sesame seeds

2 Tbs sake

2 tsp sugar

2 Tbs soy sauce

1 Tbs rice vinegar

1 pound green beans, snipped

1 tsp salt

1. Put sesame seeds in a small skillet. Toast seeds over medium heat, stirring continuously, until seeds turn lightly brown. Immediately remove seeds from pan.

2. Combine sesame seeds with remaining ingredients, except green beans and salt, in a blender. Purée until smooth, adding up to ¼ cup of water as necessary to thin the dressing.

3. Put a large skillet on the stove-top with 1 cup of water and salt. Bring to a boil, add green beans, and cook for 5 minutes, or until bright green. If using snap or snow peas cook for just 30 seconds.

4. Remove green beans from heat and toss with sesame dressing.

GREEN BEANS WITH TARRAGON

1 Tbs olive oil or butter	1 Tbs fresh tarragon leaves
1 pound green beans, trimmed	salt and pepper to taste
2 Tbs lemon juice	

1. In a large skillet, over medium high heat, melt butter or olive oil. Add green beans and toss to coat. Add ¼ cup of water and continue cooking for 4 minutes until the water has evaporated and the green beans are bright green.

2. Remove from heat. Add lemon juice and tarragon. Season to taste with salt and fresh black pepper.

BEETS AND GOAT CHEESE NAPOLEON WITH BUTTERED WALNUTS

Beets and goat cheese are a classic combination. This recipe combines the two into an impressive salad with an added depth of toasted walnuts.

1 pound red beets	1 – 2 Tbs fresh chopped thyme
2 Tbs olive oil	4 ounces creamy goat cheese
1 red onion, finely diced	Salt and pepper to taste
1 Tbs red wine vinegar	

1. Put beets in a pot and cover in cold water. Season water with salt. Bring to a boil over high heat. Reduce heat to a simmer. Continue cooking for 30 minutes, or until skins easily peel off.

2. When beets are cooked, let cool. Peel beets. Slice ¼" thick. Toss beets with red onions, vinegar, olive oil and thyme.

3. Put beets on a plate and dollop goat cheese on top. Garnish with mesclun and buttered walnuts.

BALSAMIC VINAIGRETTE AND MESCLUN

3 Tbs balsamic vinegar	½ cup + extra virgin olive oil
2 tsp chopped shallots	pinch sugar
1 tsp thyme	½ pound mesclun or lettuces
1 tsp mustard	salt and pepper to taste

4. Put balsamic, shallots, thyme and mustard in a blender. Purée. With the motor running, slowly drizzle in the oil. Season to taste with salt, pepper and sugar.

5. Use this to taste to dress the mesclun or lettuce. Left-over dressing will keep for several weeks in the fridge.

BUTTERED WALNUTS
1 cup walnuts
2 or more Tbs butter
salt and pepper

1. Melt butter in skillet. Toss in walnuts and toast until lightly browned and fragrant.

2. Season with salt and pepper.

BEET HORSERADISH SALAD

6 medium beets	2 tsp prepared horseradish
¼ cup red wine vinegar	3 scallions, chopped
½ cup olive oil	salt and pepper to taste
2 tsp sugar	

1. Put beets in a pot and cover with cold water by 1 inch. Bring to a boil, and reduce heat to simmer. Cook beets for 20 minutes, or until tender: a paring knife can be easily inserted.

2. Drain beets and let cool.

3. When beets are cool enough to handle, peel and slice them.

4. Toss beets with remaining ingredients. Season to taste with salt and pepper. Let stand for at least 20 minutes to let the flavors marry, though overnight would be ideal.

BEET RISOTTO

3 cups chicken or vegetable stock
4 Tbs whole butter
1 large shallot, diced
¾ cup Arborio rice
¼ cup white wine

1 ½ cup raw diced beets
(approximately 2 beets, peeled first)
⅓ cup Parmesan
lemon juice, salt and pepper to taste

1. Bring chicken stock to a boil. Keep hot while making the risotto

2. Heat large sauté pan over medium-high heat. Add half of the butter. When it is melted, add shallots, and sweat for 2 minutes. Add rice, stirring to ensure each grain is coated in butter.

3. Add the wine to the pan. When the rice has absorbed the wine, add ½ cup of the stock and beets. Gently stir, to ensure that nothing is sticking to the bottom of the pan. Add ½ cup of remaining liquid. Cook rice, uncovered and without stirring, until most of the liquid is absorbed. Add remaining liquid, ½ cup at a time, and continue cooking in the same method.

4. Test risotto to ensure that it is cooked almost completely. If not add more hot water, and continue cooking. Otherwise, season with salt and pepper. Stir in Parmesan and butter. Adjust seasoning with fresh lemon juice, if desired.

MOROCCAN STYLE BEET SALAD WITH MINT

6 baby beets or 3 medium beets
3 Tbs extra virgin olive oil
½ tsp ground cumin
¼ tsp ground coriander

salt, pepper and lemon juice to taste
8 large mint leaves, cut into thin strips

1. Put beets in a pot of cold water. Bring to a boil over high flame. Cover pot and let simmer for 20 minutes, or until beets are tender – a paring knife will insert easily.

2. Remove beets from heat and let cool. The skins should peel off easily.

3. Cut beets into eighths.

4. Heat olive oil in a skillet over medium flame. Add cumin, coriander, salt and pepper. Cook until spices become aromatic, about 2 minutes. Add the beets, and warm through, tossing to coat in scented oil.

5. Remove from heat and serve. Sprinkle mint on top, and a squeeze of lemon.

VARIATION: add cooked potatoes and/or carrots to this salad.

ROASTED BEETS WITH ONIONS AND BACON

Roasting beets intensifies the flavors and the sweetness. It also makes peeling easier.

4 medium sized beets
2 Tbs olive oil
1 slice bacon, diced

1 small onion, peeled and finely diced
salt and pepper to taste

1. Scrub the beets well to remove all the dirt. Toss them, unpeeled, in olive oil, wrap in foil, and bake in a 425°F oven for 30 minutes. To test for doneness, a paring knife should insert easily.

2. Let beets cool slightly. Peel with a paring knife or butter knife. Cut into quarters and set aside.

3. In a small skillet, add bacon. Cook over medium heat, stirring occasionally until bacon starts to release its fat. Drain all but 1 Tbs. Add onions and cook until soft.

4. Toss beets with bacon and onions. Season to taste with salt and pepper.

BROCCOLI MASALA

This is a variation on the Indian Cauliflower Masala. It can also be prepared with cauliflower – increase the cooking time to 15 minutes.

3 Tbs clarified butter or olive oil
½ tsp brown mustard seed
½ tsp ground cumin
pinch fenugreek
½ tsp ground turmeric
1 Tbs fresh ginger, minced
2 cloves garlic, finely chopped
1 onion, finely sliced

1 pound broccoli, separated into florets
1 small tomato, chopped
1 fresh green chili, sliced
½ tsp salt

1. Heat butter in a large skillet over medium heat, and fry mustard seeds until they start to pop. Add cumin, fenugreek, turmeric, ginger, garlic and onions. Cook, stirring frequently, until onions are soft.

2. Add broccoli, and stir until well coated. Add tomato, chili and salt, and cook until broccoli is bright green, about 3 minutes. If pan seems dry, add ¼ cup of water.

BROCCOLI WITH LEMON ZEST AND PARMESAN

1 pound broccoli
1 Tbs olive oil
2 cloves garlic, chopped
1 lemon, zest

¼ cup grated Parmesan or Romano cheese
salt and pepper to taste

1. Trim tough stalks off broccoli and cut into florets.

2. Heat a large skillet over high heat. Add oil and then garlic. Cook for 2 minutes.

3. Add broccoli and ¼ cup of water. Season with salt and pepper. Cook for 5 minutes, uncovered, stirring every so often, until broccoli is bright green.

4. Just before serving, toss with lemon zest and Parmesan cheese.

ROASTED BROCCOLI WITH CHILI FLAKES AND PARMESAN

This can be served as a side dish to roast chicken or tossed with buttered noodles for a simple supper.

2 Tbs olive oil

1 Tbs chopped garlic

¼ tsp chili flakes (optional)

1 head broccoli, cut into florets

1 squeeze lemon juice

1 – 2 Tbs freshly grated Parmesan

salt and pepper to taste

1. Heat a large skillet over high heat. Add olive oil, then garlic and chili flakes. When garlic starts to brown add broccoli. Stir to coat in olive oil and garlic.

2. Add ¼ cup of water to steam broccoli. When water evaporates and broccoli is bright green, season with salt, pepper and lemon juice.

3. Sprinkle cheese on top just before serving.

THAI RED CURRY WITH CHICKEN AND VEGETABLES

Curries are incredibly versatile; you can use whatever vegetables you have in your CSA box or find fresh at the farmers market. The key is to add the vegetables to the sauce in order of how long they take to cook. For example, carrots cook more slowly than snap peas. Use this recipe as a guide and feel free to adapt to what you have on hand.

2 cups jasmine rice

2 Tbs canola or other plain oil

2 boneless, skinless chicken breasts, sliced, sliced ¼-inch thick

½ cup chopped onion

2 Tbs red curry paste (use heaping spoons for more spicy, scant spoons for modest palate)

1 13-ounce can (unsweetened) coconut milk

2 Tbs fish sauce

1 tsp brown sugar, optional

3 cups chopped vegetables, summer or winter options (see below)

¼ cup fresh basil leaves

3 – 4 scallions, cut into long strips or rounds

salt and pepper

1. In a large sauce pan, mix rice, 1 tsp oil and 1 ½ tsp salt, ensuring to coat each grain of rice in oil. Add 3 cups of water. Bring to a boil over high heat, cover and reduce heat to low. Let cook for 10 minutes. Turn off heat and let stand for 5 more minutes, covered.

2. Meanwhile, season chicken with salt and pepper. Heat a large sauté pan over high heat. Add 1 Tbs oil, and then the chicken and onions. Stir fry for 4 minutes, remove from pan and set aside.

3. In the same pan, heat remaining oil over high heat. Add red curry paste, and stir fry for 1 minute. Add coconut milk, fish sauce (1 tsp brown sugar, if using) and any root vegetables (such as carrots, potatoes or rutabagas). Let simmer for 3-5 minutes. Add greens (broccoli, okra, cabbage, eggplant, and greens). Just when the greens turns bright green (after 1-2 minutes) add remaining vegetables (such as tomatoes, bell peppers and summer squash) and chicken. Cook for 1 minute more until everything is heated through

4. Serve curry over rice. Garnish with scallions.

SUMMER VEGETABLE OPTIONS: (total 3 cups, chopped) tomatoes, bell peppers, okra, potatoes, squash and/or eggplant.

WINTER VEGETABLES OPTIONS: (total 3 cups, chopped) sweet potatoes, turnips, carrots, radishes, broccoli, rutabagas, cabbage and/or greens.

BROCCOLI RAAB WITH HONEY AND GRAPES

The sweetness of the grapes balances nicely with the bitterness of the raab. This is a wonderful side dish for grilled lamb or quail.

1 bunch broccoli raab	½ tsp ground cumin
2 tsp olive oil	1 cup grapes, cut in half
1 garlic clove, minced	2 Tbs honey
¼ tsp chili flakes or allepo pepper	salt and pepper, taste

1. Trim the ends off the broccoli raab, and coarsely chop. Wash.

2. Heat a large skillet over high heat. Add the oil. Add the garlic and cook for 2 minutes or until aromatic. Add the spices and cook for 1 minute more to toast them before adding the raab.

3. Cook the raab, stirring frequently until it turns bright green. If the pan seems dry, add ¼ cup of water.

4. Stir in the grapes and honey. Season with salt.

BROCCOLI RAAB WITH SAUSAGE AND PASTA

1 Tbs olive oil
1 pound sweet Italian sausage, sliced
2 garlic cloves, chopped
1 bunch broccoli raab
½ tsp chili flakes

¾ pound pasta – penne or linguine or other favorite shape
¼ cup freshly grated Parmesan
salt, pepper and lemon juice to taste

1. Wash broccoli raab and coarsely chop.

2. Heat a large skillet over high heat. Add half the olive oil and sausage. Cook sausage until it starts to brown. Remove from skillet and set aside.

3. To the same pan, add the remaining olive oil, garlic and cook over medium heat until it starts to brown. Add the broccoli raab and chili flakes, and cook for 2 minutes more, or just until it turns bright green. Stir occasionally.

4. Meanwhile, bring a large pot of water to a boil. Season with salt and cook pasta according to package directions.

5. When pasta is done, strain the water, reserving about ¼ cup.

6. Toss pasta with sausage, raab and cheese. If it seems dry, add some pasta water (or extra virgin olive oil).

7. Season to taste with salt, pepper and lemon juice.

BROCCOLI RAAB WITH TOASTED SESAME SEEDS AND GINGER

2 tsp raw sesame seeds	1 bunch broccoli raab
1 tsp sesame oil	1 Tbs sake or mirin
1 clove garlic, chopped	1 tsp butter (optional)
1 tsp fresh ginger, chopped	1 tsp soy sauce

1. In a dry skillet, over medium heat, toast sesame seeds until golden brown. Immediately add sesame oil and garlic. Sauté until garlic just starts to brown.

2. Add ginger, and cook for 10 seconds. Add the raab. Then add the sake and soy sauce. Cook until just barely wilted. Remove from heat. Stir in butter.

3. If weather conditions make the raab slightly bitter, a touch of honey or sugar add with the greens can make the dish more balanced.

BRUSSELS SPROUTS "CARBONARA"

This variation on the traditional Italian dish uses Brussels sprouts instead of spring peas. You can use bacon, pancetta, turkey bacon or chicken to give a little meaty flavor to the dish.

1 pint Brussels sprouts
2 slices bacon, 2 boneless chicken thighs, smoked, or 2 Tbs olive oil
¾ pound pasta
2 garlic cloves, chopped
pinch chili flakes

¼ cup cream
¼ cup freshly grated Parmesan cheese, or more to taste
salt, pepper and lemon juice to taste

1. Preheat the oven to 425°F. Bring a large pot of water to a boil. Season generously with salt.

2. Meanwhile, cut Brussels in half. Toss them with bacon (or olive oil, if using), salt and pepper. Put them in the oven to roast for 15 minutes.

3. Boil pasta for 1 minute less than the package instructions.

4. After the Brussels have roasted 15 minutes, toss them with garlic and chili flakes. Return to oven for an additional 5 minutes to toast the garlic.

5. Drain pasta. Toss with cream, Parmesan. Add chopped smoked chicken (if using) and Brussels. Adjust seasoning with salt, pepper and lemon juice, to taste.

ROASTED BRUSSELS SPROUTS WITH BALSAMIC AND OLIVE OIL

1 pint Brussels sprouts

¼ cup extra virgin olive oil

2 Tbs balsamic vinegar

½ tsp salt

fresh cracked black pepper

1. Preheat oven to 400°F.

2. Trim the ends off the Brussels sprouts, and cut them in half.

3. Toss in a bowl with enough olive oil to coat evenly, then add balsamic vinegar, salt and pepper to taste.

4. Lightly oil a sheet pan. Spread out Brussels sprouts in a single layer (use two sheet pans if necessary, if the sprouts are crowded, they won't brown well), cut side down. Roast in oven for 15 minutes, flip the sprouts to cut side up, and then roast for about 10 minutes more or until gently browned.

QUINOA WITH ROASTED BRUSSELS SPROUTS

It's very important to rinse quinoa before cooking as the grains often have a bitter residue on them that comes from processing.

½ cup quinoa
½ pound Brussels sprouts
2 Tbs olive oil
3 cloves garlic, sliced thin or chopped

½ lemon
salt and pepper to taste
OPTIONAL: ¼ cup toasted, slivered almonds

1. Put quinoa in a fine mesh strainer and rinse under cold water. Put in a small sauce pot and cover with water by 1 inch. Add 1 tsp salt. Cover the pot and cook over medium heat for 10 minutes, or until quinoa has popped and is cooked through.

2. Meanwhile, cut Brussels sprouts in half and then slice thin.

3. Heat a large skillet over high heat. Add the olive oil, and let heat for 1 minute. Add the garlic and cook for 3 minutes or until aromatic. Add the Brussels sprouts and cook, stirring regularly, until they are bright green and soft. Remove from heat.

4. When quinoa is cooked, drain excess water. Toss with Brussels. Add juice from ½ lemon and season to taste with salt and pepper. Stir in almonds, if using.

ROASTED SWEET POTATOES AND BRUSSELS SPROUTS WITH BACON AND SAGE

2 slice bacon

1 ½ pounds sweet potatoes

1 pint Brussels sprouts, cut in half

2 Tbs olive oil

salt and pepper

½ cup fried sage leaves (page 194)

1. Dice bacon. Put in an ovenproof dish and into a 425°F oven.

2. Meanwhile, peel and cube sweet potato.

3. Toss sweet potatoes with bacon, season with salt and pepper, and return to oven. Roast until browned and soft, about 20 minutes.

4. In a separate pan, toss Brussels sprouts with olive oil, salt and pepper. Roast in the oven for 15 minutes, or until tender and caramelized on the bottom.

5. Mix the two together. Garnish with fried sage.

BRAISED GREEN CABBAGE WITH APPLES

1 small head green cabbage	2 Tbs butter
1 apple	¼ cup cider, still, sparkling or
1 small onion	slightly spiked (5% alcohol content)
1 clove garlic	salt and pepper to taste

1. Cut the cabbage in half and cut out the core. Cut into 1-inch chunks.

2. Peel the apple (though not necessary), core and chop. Peel and chop the onion. Chop the garlic clove.

3. In a large skillet, over medium heat, melt the butter. Add the onions and garlic and cook for 3 minutes, just until they soften.

4. Add the cabbage and apple. Cook for a few minutes, stirring to mix well. Add the cider and cover the pan.

5. Cook over medium low heat for 20 minutes. Season to taste with salt and pepper.

BRAISED RED CABBAGE

2 slices bacon (optional) or 2 Tbs butter

1 onion

¼ cup red wine

¼ cup red wine vinegar

1 Tbs red currant or raspberry jelly

1 Tbs sugar

1 small red cabbage, cut in half, core removed and sliced thin

1 apple, cored and chopped

salt and pepper to taste

1. In a medium pan, render bacon fat over medium heat for about 3 minutes. Add the onions and cook until onions are soft, about 5 minutes.

2. Add red wine, red wine vinegar, sugar, red currant jelly, sugar, cabbage and apple. Stir well to combine everything. Cover and cook for 20 minutes, or until cabbage is nice and tender.

3. Remove cover and continue cooking until most of the liquid has evaporated.

4. Set aside in a warm place until ready to serve.

ASIAN RED CABBAGE SLAW

½ red cabbage
6 scallions
2 Tbs canola oil
1 Tbs sesame oil
¼ cup sliced almonds

¼ cup raw sesame seeds
1 Tbs sugar
1 tsp salt
2 – 3 Tbs rice vinegar

1. Cut the core out of the cabbage and slice as thinly as possible

2. Julienne the scallions. Put in a mix bowl with the cabbage.

3. Heat the oils in a skillet over medium heat. Add the almonds and sesame seeds. Cook, stirring frequently until the nuts begin to brown. Immediately pour over the cabbage.

4. To the cabbage, add the sugar, salt and vinegar. Mix well. Let sit for 10 minutes so the flavors can meld.

FRESH KIM CHI

Kim chi is typically fermented for several days or weeks, giving it a pungent aroma. This version can be prepared in only a few hours and has a more mild flavor.

1 head white cabbage, 2 large bunches bok choy or tat soi, coarsely chopped

1 daikon, peeled and shredded

1 bunch scallions, chopped

1 ½ Tbs sugar

1 cup chicken or beef broth

1 Tbs chopped garlic

3 Tbs ground Korean (or regular) chilies

salt

1. Mix the cabbage with about 2 Tbs salt, and put in a stainless steel bowl. Put a plate on top and weigh it down to extract the excess liquid. Let sit for at least one hour, or as long as 24.

2. Rinse the cabbage, and mix with remaining ingredients.

3. Refrigerate at least two hours before serving.

HALUSHKI

This version of this superb comfort food hails from Pittsburgh.

one – 16 ounce package wide egg noodles

¼ cup bacon fat; chicken fat; or leftover ham or bacon + 1 Tbs butter

2 large onions, sliced

3 cloves garlic, chopped

½ head green cabbage, thinly sliced

1 tsp salt

½ tsp black pepper

1. Cook noodles according to package directions. Drain well.

2. Add fat and/or meat to a skillet over low heat. Add the onions and garlic. Sauté until soft.

3. Add cabbage, salt and pepper. Stir often. Once the cabbage is soft, add noodles and stir until well mixed.

4. Reheated, this makes great leftovers.

VEGETARIAN OR VEGAN OPTION: use 1 stick butter or 3 Tbs olive oil instead of bacon fat

GREENS SUBSTITUTIONS: use instead of the cabbage: 1 – 2 gallons washed kale, collards or Swiss chard, coarsely chopped

MEXICAN RED CABBAGE SLAW

¼ cup mayonnaise

⅓ cup sour cream

½ tsp ground cumin

1 chipotle pepper (canned and packed in adobo juice) or ¼ ground chipotle powder

2 cups shredded red cabbage or lettuce

2 ripe tomatoes, coarsely chopped

¼ cup finely sliced red onion

1 jalapeño, deseeded and minced (omit if you prefer mild)

¼ cup chopped cilantro

salt and lime to taste

1. In a large bowl, mix together the mayonnaise, sour cream, cumin and chipotle.

2. Toss in cabbage, tomatoes, red onion, jalapeno, garlic and cilantro. Season to taste with salt and lime juice.

SMOKY COLESLAW

Most slaw recipes start with a base of cabbage, but consider it just a canvas to express your creativity. This is a basic recipe but feel free to make it your own by adding more variety of vegetables (green beans, bell peppers or tomatoes) and other seasonings, such as blue cheese or caraway seeds.

1 small head of cabbage	1 tsp sugar
2 carrots	½ tsp celery seed or one celery
1 red onion	stalk, finely chopped
½ cup mayonnaise	1 chipotle pepper
3 Tbs cider vinegar	salt and pepper to taste

1. Using a food processor with the shredder attachment, thinly slice the cabbage, carrots and onion. Alternatively, finely chop vegetables with a sharp knife.

2. In a large bowl, combine the remaining ingredients to create the dressing. Adjust seasoning with salt and pepper.

3. Add the shredded vegetables to the dressing. Mix well to evenly coat and distribute the dressing. Let sit for one hour before serving.

CANTALOUPE SALSA I

This salsa is a wonderful accompaniment to grilled fish, such as tuna or mahi-mahi. Cous cous would be a good side dish. The recipe also works well with honeydew melons (or a combination).

¾ cup coarsely chopped cantaloupe
¼ cup chopped onion
2 Tbs chopped fresh cilantro
2 tsp olive oil

1 Tbs fresh lime juice
1 tsp minced deseeded jalapeño chili

Mix everything together. Season with salt, if desired.

CANTALOUPE SALSA II

½ cantaloupe
1 cucumber
1 small onion
1 Tbs fresh mint or cilantro – or combination of the two

1 tsp fresh ginger, chopped
1 lime, juiced
salt and pepper to taste
½ tsp sriracha or 1 small chili, minced

1. Peel and deseed cantaloupe, and cut into a fine dice. If using a large cucumber with tough skin (or a commercial, waxed cucumber), peel cucumber. Scoop out the seeds. Chop fine. Dice the onion and herbs.

2. Mix cantaloupe, onion, cucumber, ginger and herbs together. Season with lime juice, salt, pepper and chili paste if desired.

3. Serve with grilled tuna or salmon.

FRUIT SALSA

This is a raw fruit relish that goes very well with broiled, steamed, or fried fish; with chicken breast; with barbecue; or alongside vegetable salads. Let sit for an hour before serving to let the flavors develop. Does not keep, even refrigerated, for longer than 36 hours.

The salsa is designed to have as much sour flavor as sweet, so really sweet fruits like watermelon have to be supplemented with lime juice or a touch of vinegar.

3 cups chopped fruit: any combination of cantaloupe, watermelon, apples, nectarines or honeydew, deseeded and cubed into ¼ – ½-inch pieces

2 cloves garlic, chopped

3 Tbs onion, finely chopped

1 – 2 Tbs cilantro, chopped finely

1 tsp salt

1 – 2 dashes hot sauce

lime juice or vinegar, to taste

OPTIONAL: 1 chili pepper, finely chopped

Mix the above, cover tightly and refrigerate. Then taste one hour later for final seasoning. Typical serving size over fish is 2-3 tablespoons.

CARAMELIZED CARROTS WITH HONEY

1 pound carrots (peeling optional)	1 Tbs white wine
½ tsp salt	1 Tbs butter
water	¼ tsp white or black pepper
2 tsp honey	OPTIONAL: 1 tsp lemon juice

1. Leave carrots whole if they are small, or cut into 1-inch pieces.

2. Put carrots in a pot with salt and add enough cold water to barely cover.

3. Cover pot and simmer carrots until just tender.

4. Drain all but ¼ cup of water from carrots, stir in honey until fully dissolved. Cook uncovered under very low heat until all the water has evaporated. Toss with butter and pepper.

5. Season to taste with white wine, more salt and/or pepper. The lemon juice makes it lighter and more appropriate for serving alongside poultry, pork or lamb.

CARROTS IN BUTTER

1 pound carrots (peeling optional)	1 Tbs butter
½ tsp salt	¼ tsp white or black pepper
water	

1. Leave carrots whole if they are small, or cut into 1-inch pieces.

2. Put carrots in a pot with salt and add enough cold water to barely cover.

3. Cover pot and simmer carrots until just tender. Drain water and toss carrots with butter and pepper.

4. Season to taste with white wine, more salt and/or pepper.

5. Very good with snow peas or shelled English peas added in the last 30 seconds of cooking the carrots.

CARROT AND SEAFOOD SALAD

If serving a large crowd, you can also add quartered hard boiled eggs to this salad.

1 pound shelled, raw shrimp or sea scallops

water

½ lemon, juiced and rind reserved

1 tsp salt

¼ cup white wine

ice

2 Tbs olive oil

1 Tbs rice vinegar or cider vinegar, or to taste

1 pound peeled carrots, cut into really thin, 1 ½-inch long strips

4 scallions, chopped

4 radishes, cut in half and then sliced thin

2 Tbs fresh basil or dill, minced; or ¼ cup chopped parsley or sorrel

¼ tsp black pepper

pinch cayenne or dash of Tabasco

OPTIONAL: ¼ red onion, sliced thin, and 1 small cucumber, cut into 1 ½-inch slices

1. Put shellfish in a pot with just enough water to cover. Add lemon rind, salt and white wine. Turn on low heat and do not walk away. Cook until scallops are just white (or the shrimp is just pink), not simmering, not boiling. This keeps the shellfish the most tender. Immediately drain water, put shellfish in a colander and mix with ample ice to stop the cooking process.

2. Drain shellfish from ice.

3. Meanwhile, in a large bowl, mix together olive oil, vinegar and the juice from the ½ lemon juice. Mix in well the black pepper and cayenne.

4. Add remaining ingredients and shellfish to dressing. Toss well.

5. Fine to serve tepid, but refrigerate if you won't be serving the salad within two hours.

VIETNAMESE MEATBALLS WITH CRISPY SALAD

These meatballs also go well with the Kohlrabi Salad (page 161). To make a complete meal, serve with steamed rice.

1 head Boston lettuce or large tender Asian greens	1 small red chili
1 bunch mint and/or cilantro	2 Tbs honey
1 pound ground pork	2 Tbs canola oil
1 large shallot, peeled and diced	1 Tbs fish sauce
2 stalks lemon grass	2 Tbs brown sugar
2 garlic cloves	1 tsp salt
	1 tsp freshly ground black pepper.

1. Wash lettuce, mint and/or cilantro. Soak in salt water for 5 minutes. Drain and set aside on a serving plate.

2. Finely chop lemon grass, garlic, shallots and chilies (or grind with a food processor). Mix with ground pork. Add remaining ingredients and mix to combine. Let marinate for 10 minutes.

3. Form meat into meatballs about 1–inch in diameter. Put on a grill-rack.

4. Cook meatballs over a charcoal fire (or under a broiler) until caramelized on the outside and cooked through, about 10 minutes depending on the fire. Serve on a bed of lettuce with mint and/or cilantro, and the carrot-daikon salad.

5. To best enjoy the meatballs, wrap them in whole lettuce leaves with some fresh herbs and the salad.

CARROT–DAIKON SALAD

1 small daikon	sliced (optional
2 small carrots, peeled	2 Tbs fish sauce
1 tsp salt	1 Tbs rice vinegar
¼ cup water	1 Tbs lime juice
1 small chili, seeds removed and	3 tsp sugar

1. Thinly slice daikon and carrot. Toss with salt and let stand for 5 minutes. Rinse.

2. Heat water to a boil. Add garlic, chilies, fish sauce, vinegar, and sugar. Stir until sugar dissolves. Remove from heat and add carrots, daikon and lime juice.

FENNEL-CARROT SLAW

This raw salad is absolutely superb: refreshing, light, with clean and crisp flavors, and no aggressive fennel taste. Originally from John Campbell, a former chef of Restaurant Nora in Washington, DC.

1 large or 2 medium fennel bulbs

2 carrots, peeled

3 – 4 tsp Kosher or sea salt

juice of 1 lemon

freshly ground black pepper

1 tsp olive oil

OPTIONAL: ½ cup thinly slivered turnip

1. Slice the fennel as thinly as possible crossways, ⅛-inch to $^1/_{16}$-inch thick. The entire head and stems are usable. Reserve the frilly leaves and discard any tough parts. Grate the carrots coarsely.

2. Mix the carrots and fennel together in a bowl with the salt. Let sit 25 to 60 minutes, tossing occasionally. The salt crisps the vegetables.

3. Drain the mix and discard the salty juice that runs out. The mix may now be rinsed if you are averse to salt. Return the slaw to a bowl. Then mince some of the green fennel leaves as finely as possible. If the fennel did not come with frilly green leaves, substitute 2 tsp chopped parsley. Add these, the fresh lemon juice, the black pepper, and the olive oil to the vegetables. Toss well and chill.

4. Excellent served alongside vegetarian bean salads or pastas, or with grilled foods.

ROASTED CARROTS

This classic approach to carrots also works really well with turnips, small potatoes, rutabagas, onions or even radishes mixed into the same roasting pan. Best if roasted with a chicken or turkey on top of the carrots/veggies.

1 pound carrots	1 – 2 tsp chopped garlic
2 tsp olive or vegetable oil	½ cup chopped onion
½ tsp salt	½ tsp fresh thyme or oregano
¼ tsp black pepper	

1. Cut carrots into 1–inch chunks; skin can be left on. Drizzle oil on top, and then stir in salt and pepper.

2. Roast in a heavy pan at 400°F until the edges start to brown, about 15 - 20 minutes. Add garlic, onions and herbs.

3. Lower heat to 350°F and continue roasting until garlic has slightly browned and carrots have somewhat softened, about 8-10 minutes more.

CAULIFLOWER WITH PINE NUTS, SAFFRON AND RAISINS

Serve as a side dish, or toss with pasta.

2 Tbs raisins
½ cup warm water
¼ tsp saffron threads
2 Tbs olive oil
1 small red onion, diced
2 cloves garlic, minced
1 small tomato, chopped
1 anchovy

1 head cauliflower, cut in half, core removed, and then cut into florets 1 Tbs toasted pine nuts or almonds
1 tsp red wine vinegar
salt and pepper, Romano cheese, parsley, to taste

1. Soak raisins in ¼ cup of warm water. Steep saffron in remaining water.

2. Heat oil in a large skillet over medium heat. Add onions and garlic. Cook until soft, about 5 minutes.

3. Add tomatoes, anchovies and cauliflower. Cook for 10 minutes, stirring occasionally. Add saffron and raisins, along with their liquid. Cook for 10 more minutes or until cauliflower is tender. Add nuts.

4. Season to taste with salt, pepper, cheese, parsley and vinegar.

CAULIFLOWER – SPINACH SOUP

This soup is terrific served hot or cold.

3 Tbs butter	2 leeks, washed
1 shallot, peeled and chopped	¼ cup white wine
½ apple, peeled, cored and diced	6 cups water
1 celery stalk	1 cup spinach
4 garlic cloves	¼ cup cream (optional)
1 head cauliflower, cored and chopped	salt and pepper to taste

1. Heat a large pot over medium flame. Melt butter. Add shallots, apple, celery, garlic, cauliflower and leeks. Sauté until cauliflower begins to turn limp and brown a little. Deglaze with white wine. Cover vegetables with water, add a salt (about 1 tsp) and simmer until soft, about 20 minutes.

2. Purée soup with cream, and return all but 1 cup to pot. Season to taste with salt and pepper.

3. Purée remaining soup with spinach. Put in a separate pot.

4. To serve: ladle white vichyssoise into bowl. Ladle green vichyssoise into the center.

THAT EXTRA LOVING TOUCH:

Make vanilla oil to garnish soup: Heat ½ cup canola oil with ½ tsp curry powder and ½ vanilla bean. Simmer over low heat for 3 minutes. Let sit for 10 minutes. Leftover oil can be used to roast butternut squash or sweet potatoes.

ROASTED CAULIFLOWER

Perhaps the most simple and flavorful way to prepare cauliflower. Once it's roasted, you can simply season it with lemon juice, or toss it with pasta and cheese, capers, or bacon bits.

1 head cauliflower
2 Tbs extra virgin olive oil
generous pinch of salt and pepper

1. Preheat the oven to 400°F.

2. Cut cauliflower in half. Cut out core and break the cauliflower apart into florets.

3. Toss cauliflower with olive oil salt and pepper.

4. Put florets on a cookie sheet in a single layer. If there's a cut side, put that down. Be sure to not crowd the pan. If necessary, use two cookie sheets.

5. Roast in the oven for 25 minutes or until dark brown on the bottom of the cauliflower.

BRAISED CELERY

Often we buy a whole head of celery at the farmers' market just to use one or two stalks. Celery languishes in the crisper drawer because we don't often think of serving it as a vegetable. This is a great way to use copious amounts.

8 stalks celery, rinsed and trimmed, leaves chopped and reserved

1 Tbs unsalted butter

1 small onion, peeled and sliced

pinch Kosher salt

pinch freshly ground black pepper

½ cup chicken or beef broth

1. Peel any of the fibrous outer stalks of celery with a vegetable peeler and slice into 1-inch pieces diagonally.

2. Heat the butter in a large skillet over medium heat. Once melted, add the onion and cook for 5 minutes until soft. Add the celery, salt and pepper and cook for another 5 minutes until just beginning to soften slightly. Add the broth and stir to combine. Cover and reduce the heat to low. Cook until the celery is tender but not mushy, approximately 15 minutes.

3. Uncover and allow the celery to continue to cook for an additional 5 minutes or until the liquid has been reduced by half.

4. Transfer to a serving dish and garnish with chopped celery leaves.

CELERY SALAD

DRESSING
- 1 tsp salt
- ½ bunch celery, with leaves
- 1 onion, coarsely chopped
- 1 egg, at room temperature or slightly warmer (free-range if possible)
- 1 Tbs Dijon mustard
- 3 Tbs extra virgin olive oil
- ¼ can anchovy filets
- ½ bunch parsley
- ½ bunch basil
- 1 Tbs fresh chopped garlic
- ½ tsp black pepper
- ½ lemon, juiced (or to taste)

SALAD
- 4 large stalks of celery, sliced thin
- 2 cups of mixed greens – including romaine, arugula and/or mesclun
- ¼ cup grated Romano
- salt and pepper to taste
- croutons

1. Bring to a boil a medium pot with 2 cups of water. Season with salt. When the water boils, add the celery and onion (from the dressing list). Cook covered until the celery is almost fully soft, about 20 minutes; remove lid and continue cooking until fully soft. Drain well and reserve liquid.

2. To make the dressing: crack the egg into a food processor bowl. Run the machine until the egg is pale yellow, add the mustard and then slowly drizzle in the olive oil running the machine all the while. The mix should thicken substantially and whiten. Add the anchovies, celery, parsley, basil, garlic, black pepper and lemon juice. Continue running the machine until the dressing is smooth and creamy. Let sit for 15 minutes, pulse again, and then taste for seasoning. Excellent optional additions are white wine, cayenne or Worcestershire sauce.

3. In a large salad bowl, combine the thin slices of celery and lettuces. Add the grated Romano and toss with ¼ cup of the dressing. Remaining dressing will keep for 6 weeks.

4. Adjust seasoning. Garnish with croutons.

CELERY SOUP

A great way to tenderize tougher, late summer celery.

1 head celery, washed well
2 Tbs olive oil
1 carrot, peeled and diced
2 cloves garlic
1 onion, peeled and diced

3 cups chicken broth
½ – 1 cup cream or plain yogurt
salt, pepper and lemon juice to taste
GARNISH: chopped dill, parsley or
sweet red pepper

1. Trim leaves off celery. Cut into 1- inch pieces.

2. Heat a skillet over medium heat. Add olive oil. Then add carrots, garlic and onions. Cook for 3 minutes, or until soft.

3. Add celery to the skillet and toss to coat in oil and veggies. Add chicken broth.

4. Bring to a boil, and reduce heat to simmer. Cover and cook for 15 minutes, or until celery is tender.

5. Purée soup in a blender (be sure to crack the lid a little to let the steam escape). Add cream or yogurt. Purée again.

6. Return soup to pot and season to taste with salt, pepper and lemon juice.

7. Garnish with herbs or peppers before serving.

SPICY SHRIMP, CELERY AND CASHEW STIR-FRY

This recipe can be easily adapted to use chicken and peanuts instead of shrimp and cashews.

1 pound shrimp, peeled and cleaned

¼ tsp salt

1 tsp soy sauce

1 egg white

2 Tbs plain or peanut oil

1 Tbs ginger, peeled and finely minced

2 cloves garlic, chopped

3 scallions, cut into rounds

3 celery stalks, sliced

¾ cup roasted, salted cashews

SAUCE

½ tsp salt

1 Tbs sugar

2 Tbs Chinese black vinegar or balsamic

2 tsp Shaio Xing wine or sherry

2 Tbs water or chicken broth

1 tsp corn starch

1 – 2 tsp or more chili paste (like sriracha)

1. In a small bowl, marinate the shrimp with ¼ tsp salt, soy sauce and egg white. In a separate bowl, combine all sauce ingredients.

2. Heat a large wok or skillet over high heat until very hot, about 2 minutes. Add 1 Tbs of the oil, ginger, garlic and ½ the scallions. Let cook for 1 minute and then add the celery and cashews. Season with ¼ tsp salt, and stir-fry until the celery turns jade green, about 3 minutes. Transfer the mixture to a plate.

3. Return the skillet to high heat. Add the remaining 1 Tbs oil and shrimp and stir-fry until shrimp start to curl and turn pink, about 2 minutes. Return the celery and cashews to the pan and add the sauce. Stir over the heat for about 1 minute to mix together evenly and blend flavors. Transfer the stir-fry to a platter and garnish with the remaining scallions.

4. Serve with steamed white or brown rice.

CELERIAC PURÉE

This makes a great side dish for roasted meats or fish.

2 knobs celery root (celeriac)
½ cup cream
salt, pepper and lemon juice to taste

1. Peel celery root and cut into chunks.

2. Put celeriac in a pot and cover with cold water. Add a generous amount of salt, about 1 tablespoon per quart of water. Bring to a boil, reduce heat to simmer. Cook for about 20 minutes, or until celeriac is tender.

3. Drain the celery root and reserve 1 cup of water. Put root in a food processor and purée with cream. If it seems too thick, add some of the reserved cooking liquid. Add lemon juice, 1 squeeze at a time, until it is seasoned to your taste. Adjust seasoning with salt and pepper.

CELERIAC RÉMOULADE

A variant on cole slaw, rémoulade makes a great side dish for crab cakes or grilled fish.

¼ cup mayonnaise

1 Tbs minced fresh parsley leaves

2 tsp fresh lemon juice

½ tsp drained bottled capers, minced

1 tsp Dijon mustard

1 tsp fresh tarragon, minced, or ¼ tsp dried

2 small celeriac, peeled and cut into matchstick pieces or shredded coarse

1. In a small bowl combine ingredients for dressing: mayonnaise, parsley, lemon juice, capers, mustard, tarragon, and salt and pepper to taste. Mix until combined well. Toss with celery root.

2. Chill until ready to serve.

BEEF ROULADE WITH CILANTRO MOJO

2 red bell peppers, quartered, seeds removed	2 carrots, peeled and thinly sliced
2 stalks thyme	1 stick butter, cut into chunks
5 cloves garlic	4 sweet potatoes, peeled and chunked
1 tsp cayenne or chili flakes	2 slices ginger
1 cup extra virgin olive oil	¼ cup cream
2 pounds flank steak	1 Tbs plain oil
1 Tbs fresh oregano	1 bunch watercress
1 lime, juiced	salt, pepper and lemon juice to taste

1. To a large sauce pot, add red peppers, thyme, garlic cloves smashed and cayenne. Cover with olive oil. Simmer over medium heat for 15 minutes, or until peppers are tender. Let cool.

2. Season steak with salt (1 ½ tsp), pepper (½ tsp), oregano and lime juice. Rub meat with roasted garlic. Lay out steak, and place red peppers and carrots on top. Dot with butter. Roll steak with the grain, and tie with kitchen string.

3. Put sweet potatoes and ginger in a pot of salted water and bring to a boil. Reduce heat to a simmer and continue cooking until potatoes are tender. Drain water and purée potatoes with cream. Season with salt, pepper and lemon juice. Set aside in a warm place until ready to serve.

4. Heat oil in a pan. Brown meat on all sides, and finish cooking in the oven for about 10 minutes for medium rare. Let meat rest for 10 minutes. Remove strings, and slice meat as thin as possible. Garnish with watercress, sweet potatoes and cilantro mojo.

CILANTRO MOJO

½ cup olive oil	2 tsp pepper
¼ cup chopped garlic	1 Tbs salt
½ cup chopped onion	1 cup white vinegar
2 tsp ground cumin	1 ½ cups cilantro, leaves and stems
1 Tbs fresh oregano	

1. Heat olive oil over medium heat. Add garlic, onions, cumin and oregano. Cook for 3 minutes, or until garlic becomes aromatic.

2. Strain olive oil and reserve. Purée garlic onion mixture with remaining ingredients. Slowly whisk in olive oil. Adjust seasoning to taste.

CHICKEN CRIOLLO

2 ½ cups cilantro (stems and all)

1 Tbs ground cumin

1 Tbs fresh oregano

2 tsp salt

1 Tbs ground black pepper

¾ cup coarsely chopped onion

⅓ cup coarsely chopped garlic

1 ⅓ cup vinegar

¼ cup oil

2 chickens, cut into pieces

additional salt and pepper to taste

1. Combine all ingredients, except chicken, in a blender.

2. Season chicken with salt and pepper. Marinate chicken in above mixture for at least 30 minutes and up to two days (the longer the better).

3. Bake chicken in the marinade at 350°F for 20-30 minutes or until cooked through. Serve with rice.

CORN FRITTERS WITH RED PEPPER SALSA

2 slices bacon, diced

¼ cup diced red onion

3 ears corn, kernels cut off cob

½ cup red pepper, diced

¼ cup diced scallions or chives

½ cup corn meal

1 ½ cup flour

1 Tbs baking powder

¼ tsp cayenne pepper (optional)

1 cup milk

2 eggs

salt and pepper to taste

canola oil for frying

1. In a large skillet, cook bacon until half crisp. Add onions and corn, and cook until onions are soft. Cool mixture. Add red peppers and scallions. Season with salt and pepper to taste.

2. In a bowl, mix dry ingredients together (corn meal, flour, baking powder, cayenne pepper and salt). Make a well in the center and add the milk and eggs. Stir just to incorporate all ingredients.

3. Combine corn mixture with batter, and stir to mix everything together.

4. Fry 2 Tbs of batter per fritter in oil that is over a medium-high flame until golden brown on all sides. Drain on paper towel. Serve with salsa (or chipotle aioli, see Vegetarian Cuban Sandwich recipe, page 203).

RED PEPPER SALSA

1 large tomato

½ red onion

2 cloves garlic (optional)

4 scallions, cut into rounds

2 red chili peppers, or 1 canned chipotle pepper

2 sweet red peppers

4 Tbs cilantro, chopped, or to taste

2 Tbs extra virgin olive oil

2 limes juiced, or to taste

salt to taste

Chop vegetables. Mix together with everything else. Adjust seasoning to taste.

CORN AND TOMATO SUCCOTASH

There's no "right" recipe for succotash, you can use whatever summer vegetables you have on hand. Simply seasoned with basil and lemon juice, there's nothing better!

1 medium tomato	2 ears corn
1 small onion	1 ½ Tbs olive oil or butter
2 cloves garlic	lima or butter beans, if available
1 zucchini or yellow squash	1 Tbs fresh basil
1 small red bell pepper	salt, pepper and lemon juice to taste

1. Prepare vegetables: Chop tomato. Dice onion, chop garlic, dice zucchini and bell pepper. Cut corn kernels from cob.

2. In a heavy skillet, heat butter over medium-high heat. Add the corn in a single layer and sprinkle the onions and garlic on top. Do not stir for a few minutes until the corn develops a sweet, roasted aroma. Stir, and continue cooking for 1 minute.

3. Add the squash, pepper and lima beans, stirring occasionally, until the squash is bright, about 3 minutes. Stir in tomato and basil and simmer, stirring occasionally, 2 minutes, until everything is heated through.

4. Season with salt, pepper and lemon juice to taste.

CREAMY CORN CHOWDER

5 ears corn
1 pint light cream
1 pint chicken stock
3 large onions
¼ cup salt pork or bacon, diced
(vegetarian option: 2 Tbs butter)
2 cloves garlic

1 Tbs butter
2 small new potatoes, cut into small
dice, and par-cooked (about ½ cup)
4 scallions, cut into rings

1. Remove corn kernels from cob. Place cobs in a large pot with cream and chicken stock. Simmer over medium heat for 20 minutes. Remove cobs, scraping out the juices with a butter knife. Discard the cobs.

2. Cut onions in ½ along the poles. Place them on a greased cookie sheet (or Pyrex dish), cut side down. Roast in 400°F oven for 40 minutes, or until tender. Scoop out inner part of the onion (leaving the 3 outer rings that create a cup) and add to corn stock. Reserve outer part of the onion for serving.

3. In a large pan, over medium heat, cook the salt pork or bacon until about 1 Tbs of fat releases. Add garlic and ½ of corn. Cook until garlic is lightly browned. Add to above corn stock.

4. Purée soup in a blender or with an immersion blender. Season to taste with salt and pepper.

5. Prepare garnish for soup: Heat a large sauté pan over medium flame. Add butter and let melt. Add potatoes and corn. Sauté until potatoes begin to crisp. Turn off heat and stir in scallions rounds.

6. To serve: place an onion cup in each soup bowl, and ladle soup inside onion cup; it's okay if the soup spills out of the onion into the bowl. Top with garnish.

FETTUCCINE WITH BACON, GREENS AND SWEET CORN

A sauceless pasta, light and full of flavor. Traditionally one type of "Pasta Asciutta."

2 – 3 Tbs olive oil

1 onion, sliced thin

2 red bell peppers or 8 slender Italian seasoning peppers, sliced thin

3 cloves garlic, chopped

½ pound bacon, chopped, fully cooked and drained; or 1 can black beans, drained and rinsed.

3 ears corn, kernels removed

½ gallon washed arugula, or 1 gallon mustard greens, kale, Swiss chard or collard greens

1 pound box penne, rigatoni or fettuccine pasta

½ cup fresh basil, coarsely chopped

4 ounces Romano or Parmesan cheese, grated

salt and pepper to taste

1. In a large skillet, over medium-high heat, add olive oil. Sauté onions, peppers, garlic until the onions are just translucent, about 4 minutes. Add bacon (or black beans), corn, salt and pepper. Cook 1 more minute. Set aside while cooking the pasta.

2. Cook the pasta in boiling salted water according to package directions.

3. Return the onion/veggie pan to heat, and add the greens. Cook just until the greens are wilted, 1 – 2 minutes. Remove from heat and toss basil, veggies and pasta all together.

4. Sprinkle cheese on top when serving.

BASIC POPCORN

1 3 – quart covered saucepan	2 Tbs or more (to taste) of butter
3 Tbs canola oil	OPTIONAL: 2 Tbs diced fresh chilies,
⅓ cup popcorn kernels	2 strips (raw) bacon, diced
salt to taste	

1. Heat the oil in a 3–quart saucepan on medium high heat.

2. Put 3 or 4 popcorn kernels into the oil and cover the pan.

3. When the kernels pop, remove pan from heat. Add the rest of the kernels in an even layer, a generous pinch of salt, as well as either (or both) of the optional additions. Cover.

4. Return the pan to the heat. The popcorn should begin popping soon, and all at once. Once the popping starts in earnest, gently shake the pan by moving it back and forth over the burner. Try to keep the lid slightly ajar to let the steam from the popcorn release (the popcorn will be drier and crisper). Once the popping slows to several seconds between pops, remove the pan from the heat, remove the lid, and dump the popcorn immediately into a wide bowl.

5. If you are using butter, place it in the now empty, but hot pan to melt. When melted, pour over popcorn.

KETTLE POPCORN

1 3 – quart covered saucepan | salt to taste
3 Tbs canola oil | 2 Tbs or more (to taste) of butter
⅔ cup popcorn kernels
⅔ cup white sugar

1. Heat the oil in a 3-quart saucepan on medium high heat.

2. Put 3 or 4 popcorn kernels into the oil and cover the pan.

3. When the kernels pop, remove pan from heat. Add the rest of the kernels in an even layer, plus a generous pinch of salt and the sugar. Cover.

4. Return the pan to the heat, and give it a good shake. The popcorn should begin popping soon, and all at once. Once the popping starts in earnest, gently shake the pan by moving it back and forth over the burner. Once the popping slows to several seconds between pops, remove the pan from the heat, remove the lid, and dump the popcorn immediately into a wide bowl.

COLD CUCUMBER SOUP

This soup keeps very well, so you can make a big batch to serve for several meals. Perfect for extended heat waves. Very good served with thin, crisp crackers.

6 large cucumbers, peeled, seeded and very coarsely chopped

1 quart plain, non-fat (or full fat) yogurt

½ lemon, juiced

1 Tbs olive oil

½ yellow onion, coarsely chopped

½ tsp salt

½ tsp black pepper

¼ cup basil leaves

GARNISH: chopped parsley, scallion, basil or dill

1. In a blender, combine cucumber, yogurt, lemon juice and olive oil. Purée until just a little texture remains. It may be necessary to blend in several batches.

2. Leave 1 cup of cucumber purée in blender, and add onion. Purée until smooth. Then add salt, pepper and basil and pulse until the basil is just chopped.

3. Refrigerate for 1 hour and then taste for seasoning – you may want to add more salt, lemon juice, herbs, a dash of white wine or beer.

4. Garnish with additional herbs.

COOL CRUNCHY CUCUMBER SALAD

The vegetables in this salad are cut into long strips. This allows the dressing to season them in short order. If you choose to cut the vegetables larger, let sit for at least one hour before serving.

1 rib celery, julienned

1 pear, julienned

2 small carrots, peeled and julienned

1 cucumber, peeled and julienned

6 scallions, julienned

1 ½ tsp vinegar

1 ½ tsp lemon juice

2 tsp sugar

1 Tbs sesame oil

½ tsp salt

Mix everything together.

ISRAELI SALAD WITH CUCUMBERS AND DILL

2 of your favorite heirloom tomatoes
3 small cucumbers
1 red bell pepper or mildly hot red pepper
3 scallions
3 Tbs extra virgin olive oil

1 Tbs lemon juice
1 ½ Tbs fresh dill
½ tsp salt
¼ tsp freshly ground black pepper

1. Coarsely chop tomatoes. Toss with salt and pepper. Let sit for 10 minutes.

2. Meanwhile, coarsely chop cucumbers (unpeeled) and red peppers.

3. Drain excess liquid from tomatoes. Toss with remaining ingredients. Adjust seasoning to taste with salt, pepper, lemon and/or olive oil.

MEXICAN CUCUMBER AND JICAMA SALAD

Excellent in the heat of summer. Great with vegetarian burritos or grilled fish.

1 jicama (slightly bigger than baseball-size), peeled and cut into 2–inch x ¼–inch strips

3 large or 4 medium cucumbers, cut in half, deseeded if desired and then cut into 2–inch strips

½ yellow or red onion, sliced thinly

1 clove garlic, chopped fine

1 lime, juiced

1 – 2 Tbs olive oil

½ tsp salt

4 Tbs cilantro, leaves torn, or 1 Tbs basil – either lime or lemon

½ tsp dried red chili flakes or ½ jalapeno pepper, minced

Mix everything together. Refrigerate at least 10 minutes before serving.

MINT AND CUCUMBER RAITA

This makes a wonderful condiment to grilled beef, lamb kebobs, or grilled vegetables

1 cup plain, non-fat yogurt

1 Tbs fresh chopped mint

½ cucumber, peeled, seeded and chopped

¼ lemon, juiced

1 garlic clove, chopped

¼ tsp salt

pepper to taste

Mix everything together.

PICKLES

BREAD AND BUTTER

These pickles have a sweet and sour flavor. They are great in sandwiches or chopped up in tuna or egg salad. Properly stored in the fridge, they will keep up to six months.

4 small firm cucumbers, sliced into
½ -inch wheels

4 cups water

¼ cup salt

1 ½ cups cider vinegar

1 ¼ cups sugar

1 Tbs mustard seeds

1 celery stalk

¼ tsp turmeric

⅛ tsp ground clove

⅛ tsp ground ginger

black pepper, freshly ground

Put everything (including cucumber slices) in a stainless steel (or non-reactive) pot. Bring to a boil, stirring frequently to dissolve the sugar. Reduce heat to low and simmer for 20 minutes. Store pickles in this liquid in the refrigerator.

HALF-SOUR DILL PICKLES

medium cucumbers

1 bunch dill

fresh garlic cloves, crushed

black pepper

salt

1. Slice cucumbers into sixths, lengthwise, to yield long spears.

2. Put them in a stainless steel bowl. Cover with cold water. Pour water out into a big bowl, and measure. For every 2 cups of water, add 1 Tbs of salt. Stir until salt dissolves.

3. Pour salted water back over cucumber spears. Add crushed garlic, fresh dill and black pepper. Stir to distribute all the seasoning.

4. Use a plate to weight down the cucumbers so that they are completely submerged in the liquid.

5. Let sit for at least 24 hours at room temperature to ferment before storing in the fridge or canning.

SAUTÉED CUCUMBERS

These cucumbers are a perfect dish for those occasional rainy summer nights.

2 large cucumbers	1 Tbs fresh mint or dill
1 Tbs butter	salt, pepper and lemon juice to taste

1. Peel the cucumbers and slice in half lengthwise. Scoop out the seeds using a melon-baller or tsp. Cut into ½-inch slices.

2. Heat a large skillet over medium heat. Add butter and melt. Add the cucumbers and cook for 4 minutes, stirring frequently. Season with salt and pepper.

3. Remove from heat and add fresh herbs and a squeeze of fresh lemon juice.

BABA GANOUSH I

Traditionally, raw garlic is added to the dip, but Julia prefers the flavor of roasted. If you like raw garlic, reduce the quantity to one or two cloves.

4 medium eggplants	1 lemon, juiced
4 cloves garlic	salt and pepper
1 Tbs olive oil	parsley or scallions for garnish
2 Tbs tahini	
½ tsp ground cumin	

1. Prick whole eggplant with a fork. Place directly over a fire (a gas burner or grill) and cook until they are blackened on all sides and the flesh is tender. Let cool.

2. In a piece of aluminum foil, wrap up the garlic and olive oil. Roast in 350°F oven for 30 minutes, or until the garlic is soft and golden brown.

3. Peel the charred, black skin away from the eggplant and discard.

4. Put the eggplant pulp, tahini, cumin, garlic, and lemon juice in a food processor. Blend until smooth. Season to taste with salt and pepper.

5. Garnish with scallions or parsley.

BABA GANOUSH II

Adapted from Tess Mallos, The Complete Middle East Cookbook.

3 large eggplants
3 cloves garlic
⅓ cup tahini
1 – 2 Tbs olive oil
¼ – ⅓ cup fresh lemon juice
2 – 3 tsp salt, but to taste

black pepper or Tabasco to taste
¼ cup basil, herbs of Provence, or parsley
OPTIONAL: 2 Tbs freshly toasted sesame seeds

1. Bake the whole eggplant in a lightly oiled, heavy roasting pan or iron skillet at 375°F until soft. Remove from oven and peel and de-stem while still warm.

2. Purée eggplant, garlic and tahini in a Cuisinart until smooth, then drizzle in first the olive oil and then the lemon juice, with the motor running all the while.

3. Add herb(s), salt, and pepper. Adjust seasoning. Sprinkle with the freshly toasted sesame seeds.

4. Serve with crusty bread, crackers, or as a dip for raw vegetables. Keeps very well frozen if well covered. When thawed, you may find it best to add some bread crumbs to absorb the fluid that results from the freezing. Excellent to have stored in the freezer for quick entertaining or snacks.

BEEF WITH EGGPLANT

Adapted from The Chinese Kitchen *by Eileen Yin-Fei Lo, a must-have book for lovers of Chinese cooking.*

½ pound sirloin steak, cut against the grain into ¼-inch wide strips

3 tsp fresh ginger, chopped

½ tsp gin

¼ tsp salt

1 tsp canola oil

1 Tbs corn starch

2 small eggplants

1 tsp salt

2 tsp fresh garlic chopped

canola or other neutral oil for frying

scallions for garnish

SAUCE

1 Tbs Chinese bean sauce

½ cup chicken stock

2 tsp sugar

2 Tbs oyster sauce

1 tsp soy sauce

1. In a large bowl, combine the beef, 1 tsp of ginger, gin, ¼ tsp salt, 1 tsp oil and corn starch. Let beef marinate for at least 30 minutes.

2. Cut eggplant into ½-inch slices. Toss with 1 tsp salt. Let sit for 5 minutes. Rinse off salt and pat dry eggplant.

3. Mix together ingredients for sauce and set aside.

4. In a large skillet, add ¼-inch of canola oil. Heat to 350°F. Add eggplant slices and cook until deep golden brown, about 10 minutes. Drain the eggplant and set aside. Drain oil from the pan except for one tablespoon. Return pan to heat. Add the garlic and remaining ginger, and cook for 1 minute or until aromatic. Add the beef and stir-fry until the meat loses its pink edges, about 3 minutes. Add the sauce and cook until it thickens. Stir in the eggplant to coat with sauce.

5. Garnish with scallions.

CHINESE STIR-FRIED EGGPLANT

2 large Italian eggplants or 4 small
Asian eggplants
2 ½ Tbs corn starch
2 Tbs plain oil
1 Tbs fresh ginger, chopped
1 tsp fresh garlic, chopped
3 scallions, cut into rings

SAUCE:
2 Tbs oyster sauce
2 tsp dark soy sauce
1 tsp sugar
2 tsp gin
¾ cup chicken stock
1 – 2 tsp chili paste or sriracha –
depending on taste

1. Combine ingredients for sauce.

2. Cut eggplant into 1–inch cubes and toss in corn starch.

3. Heat a large skillet over high heat. Add the oil. When oil is hot, add eggplant in a single layer.

4. Cook eggplant until it starts to brown, and toss. Add ginger and garlic and cook until fragrant.

5. Stir in sauce and scallions and cook until the sauce thickens.

6. Serve over rice.

EGGPLANT CAPONATA OR RATATOUILLE

This is a great way to use up a lot of eggplant, squash, and very ripe tomatoes when the vegetable flood of summer is at peak. Caponata is wonderfully intense, and may be canned or even frozen to enjoy in autumn or winter, though a post-thaw re-seasoning is advised if freezing. Caponata is traditionally served with bread or crackers as an appetizer, as a vegetarian main course over rice, polenta, or pasta, within pizza, or in sandwiches (hot or cold). If you leave out the olives and capers, this recipe produces a version of ratatouille.

3 pounds ripe eggplant, skin on, cut in ½-inch chunks

3 medium onions, chopped

½ head garlic, chopped

¼ cup olive oil

1 cup red wine

2 tsp salt

1 – 2 tsp black pepper

4 large bell peppers, chopped

1 quart ripe or very ripe tomatoes, puréed in a blender

1 large or 2 medium summer squash

¾ cup pitted, stuffed green olives

¼ cup capers

fresh oregano, thyme, basil (about ¼ cup total), and/or fennel seed

1. Sauté the first three ingredients in the oil in a large heavy stainless pot. Use moderate heat and a lid to minimize sticking, but add water if anything starts burning.

2. Add next 4 ingredients once the eggplant has softened somewhat. Simmer 3 more minutes to slightly soften the peppers, and then add everything else but the herbs. Simmer until the squash has just softened, then remove from heat.

3. Stir in the herbs, and add more salt and/or pepper to taste.

EGGPLANT CURRY

Loosely adapted from Singapore Food *by Wendy Hutton.*

1 Tbs plain oil	½ tsp ground coriander
4 small eggplants, cut in quarters lengthwise, and then into 1 ½-inch slices	¼ tsp ground cumin
	⅛ tsp ground fennel
	¼ tsp mustard seed
1 small onion, chopped	pinch (or more) cayenne pepper
3 cloves garlic, chopped	1 cup unsweetened coconut milk
1 tsp salt	½ cup water
⅛ tsp turmeric	½ lime, juiced

1. Heat a large skillet over high heat. Add oil and then eggplant in a single layer. Let eggplant sit so that it can brown on the bottom side for about 4 minutes, then flip.

2. Add onions and garlic to the pan and continue cooking, stirring occasionally, for about 3 minutes, until onions start to soften.

3. Add spices and salt, and stir to coat eggplant.

4. Add coconut milk and water and simmer for about 10 minutes or until eggplant is tender.

5. Season with lime juice just before serving.

EGGPLANT WITH FRESH TOMATO SAUCE

6 Tbs olive oil

2 garlic cloves, chopped

1 onion, chopped

2 pounds plum tomatoes, diced

2 Tbs fresh tarragon

3 Italian eggplants, about 2 pounds

1 Tbs olive oil

1 pound fresh mozzarella cheese

salt and pepper to taste

basil to garnish

1. Heat 3 Tbs olive oil in a sauce pan. Add garlic and onions and cook until they are soft. Add tomatoes and continue cooking until most of the liquid is reduced and the sauce is thick. Stir in tarragon. Remove from heat and set aside.

2. Cut eggplant into slices. Season with salt and pepper, toss with olive oil. Broil (or grill) for 5 minutes (turning once), or until they are half soft.

3. Top eggplant with mozzarella, and some tomato sauce. Bake at 400°F for 5 minutes more, until eggplant is soft and cheese is melted.

4. Garnish with fresh basil.

EGGPLANT PARMESAN WITH SHRIMP

"Parmesan" dishes derive their name not from the namesake cheese but from the region where the dish originated: Parma. In fact, the traditional dish has a layer of Parma ham (prosciutto) and is traditionally made with veal.

1 large eggplant, sliced ½-inch

½ tsp salt

½ cup all-purpose flour

1 egg

1 cup bread crumbs

2 Tbs olive oil

1 Tbs canola oil

1 ball fresh mozzarella (about 4 ounces), sliced ¼-inch

3 garlic cloves, minced

1 small chili, minced

1 pound shrimp, peeled and deveined

¼ cup white wine

2 cups stewed tomatoes (page 222)

basil, salt and pepper

1. Toss eggplant with ½ tsp salt and let sit for five minutes. Brush off excess salt. Preheat the oven to 375°F.

2. Prepare the breading: in 3 separate bowls, put the flour, egg and bread crumbs. Beat the egg with 2 Tbs of water until well mixed.

3. Dip each eggplant slice first in the flour. Shake off any excess. Then dip into the egg to completely coat, and finally coat the eggplant in the bread crumbs. Lay breaded slices on a cookie sheet. Repeat this process with remaining slices.

4. Heat a large skillet over medium-high heat. Add 1 Tbs olive oil and canola oil. Fry the eggplant slices until brown on both sides. Don't worry if they are not cooked all the way through. Remove eggplant from skillet and put on a cookie sheet.

5. Top each eggplant with a slice of mozzarella cheese. Bake in the oven until the cheese is melted and bubbly, about 10 minutes.

6. Meanwhile, wipe out the eggplant pan. Add the remaining olive oil, garlic and chili and return to heat. Add the shrimp and cook until they begin to turn pink. Add the wine, and then the tomatoes. Remove the shrimp from the pan as they are cooked through, but continue cooking the tomatoes until they reduce until thick. Season to taste with salt, pepper and basil.

7. To serve, spoon the tomato sauce onto a serving platter and lay shrimp and eggplant slices on top.

MEDITERRANEAN EGGPLANT AND TOMATOES

Eggplants and tomato are a classic Mediterranean combination. With basil, this dish takes an Italian flair and pairs beautifully with grilled steak and potatoes. With dill, the Turkish inspiration takes over, making it perfect with mackerel and basmati rice.

¼ cup plain oil

3 medium eggplants, sliced in half lengthwise

2 Tbs currants or raisins

2 Tbs pine nuts

1 Tbs butter

1 shallot, peeled and diced

1 garlic clove, chopped

¼ cup white wine

2 cups diced tomatoes

2 Tbs fresh basil or 1 Tbs fresh dill

salt and pepper to taste

1. In a large skillet heat oil over high heat. Add eggplant to pan, cut side down, and cook until a deep brown. Flip over and cook on the other side until the eggplant is soft, about 1 more minute. It's important to cook the eggplant in a single layer, so you may need to cook them in batches. Drain on a paper towel and season with salt.

2. When eggplants are cooked, pour off the oil from the pan. Return the pan to a medium heat. Add the pine nuts and raisins and cook for 2 minutes, stirring constantly, or just until the pine nuts start to brown. Remove from heat and drain on a paper towel.

3. Wipe the pan clean, return to medium high heat, and add the butter. When the butter melts and shallots and garlic. Cook for 5 minutes, or until soft. Add the wine and reduce. Add the tomatoes. Cook until the tomatoes have released their liquid and the sauce starts to thicken. Season to taste with salt and pepper.

4. Just before serving, stir in the fresh herbs. When serving, sprinkle toasted pine nuts and currants on top.

MISO-RUBBED GRILLED EGGPLANT

Japanese eggplants have no trace of bitterness, even without salting. They cook more quickly than the conventional varieties, and the flavor is sweeter.

3 cloves garlic

3 Japanese eggplants, sliced in half lengthwise

3 Tbs olive or canola oil

1 cup white miso

½ cup sugar

¼ cup mirin (sweet rice wine)

¼ cup sake

1. Finely chop garlic. Toss eggplant with garlic and oil to marinate.

2. Combine remaining ingredients in a sauce pot. Cook over medium heat, stirring constantly until completely combined and sugar has dissolved.

3. Prepare a charcoal grill. Grill eggplant, cut side down, for 3 minutes or until lightly charred. Flip over and brush with miso paste. Cook for 2 minutes more. If you'd like, flip again to char the miso paste onto eggplant.

4. Serve with rice, shrimp or grilled corn.

MOUSSAKA

Moussaka is a layered casserole dish with origins in Greece. It reminds us of lasagna with fried eggplant slices instead of pasta, and besamel, the Greek version of béchamel.

EGGPLANT
- 3 medium sized eggplant
- 1 Tbs salt
- ½ cup flour
- ½ cup olive oil
- ½ cup grated Asiago cheese

- 1 tsp cinnamon
- ½ tsp dried Greek or regular oregano
- 2 cups puréed tomato
- salt and pepper
- 2 Tbs fresh mint

SAUCE
- 1 Tbs olive oil
- 1 onion, peeled and chopped
- 3 cloves garlic, peeled and chopped
- 1 pound ground lamb

BESAMEL SAUCE
- 2 cups milk
- 2 Tbs butter, room temperature
- ¼ cup flour
- 3 eggs
- ½ tsp salt

1. Cut the eggplant into ½-inch slices. Sprinkle them with salt and let sit for 20 minutes.

2. Meanwhile, start the sauce: Heat olive oil in a large pot. Add onions and garlic, and cook until they start to soften, about 3 minutes. Add the lamb, salt and pepper. With a spoon, break up the lamb. Add the cinnamon, oregano and tomatoes. Continue cooking until the sauce is thick, about 20 minutes. Set aside and stir in the mint.

3. Make the besamel sauce: in a pot, heat 1 ½ cups of milk. In a bowl, whisk eggs with remaining milk. Knead together the flour and butter. Slowly pour hot milk into egg/milk mixture while whisking vigorously. Return pot to medium heat. Stir in flour/butter mix and continue cooking until it thickens. Season with salt and remove from heat.

4. Fry eggplant: Brush off excess salt and moisture. Dust slices with flour. Heat a large skillet over high heat. Add the oil. When the oil starts to shimmer, fry the eggplant slices until golden brown on both sides. It may be necessary to cook in several batches. Drain on a paper towel.

5. Assemble the moussaka: in a 9-inch x 9-inch Pyrex dish, layer half of the eggplant slices on the bottom of the pan. Sprinkle about ⅓ of the cheese on top. Pour sauce on top and spread evenly in the pan. Layer the remaining eggplant on top. Sprinkle another third of the cheese

on top of the eggplant. Pour the besamel sauce on top and sprinkle remaining cheese on top of that.

6. Bake at 375°F for 30 minutes or until top is golden brown.

VIETNAMESE EGGPLANT

This recipe comes from Even' Star CSA member Mai-Liem Slade. As she writes,

"An ode my mom who passed away almost 5 years ago, the only way I was introduced to eggplant as a kid was to roast it in an oven, drench it in Vietnamese dipping sauce (nuoc mam) and served over warm jasmine rice."

2 medium eggplants	2 scallions, cut into rounds
2 – 3 Tbs neutral oil	nuoc mam sauce

1. Roast whole eggplants in 375°F oven until soft. When cool, peel the skin and use a fork to spaghetti the eggplant, then cut stem away.

2. Put eggplant in a bowl. In a skillet, heat 2-3 Tbs of oil and sauté 1-2 stems of green scallions. Pour it into the eggplant bowl.

3. Then make the fish sauce dressing as below (approximate according to taste i.e. spicy or sour):

NUOC MAM SAUCE

2 cloves of garlic	3-4 Tbs water
1-2 chili peppers	juice of half lime
3-4 Tbs fish sauce	1 tsp sugar to taste

1. Mash the garlic and peppers together (I use a mortar and pestle) to form a paste (use a little sugar so that the garlic won't jump around). Add the fish sauce, water and lime juice and sugar. Adjust the ingredients according to taste.

2. Serve eggplants over rice or onto the side and pour the fish sauce over it. Hopefully it's not too addicting. Enjoy!

FENNEL WITH RAISINS

3 fennel bulbs	1 tsp whole cumin seed
2 Tbs olive oil	¼ cup raisins
1 onion, diced	¼ chicken broth or water

1. Cut off tops of fennel. Discard or save for garnish.

2. Cut fennel, lengthwise into quarters.

3. Heat olive oil over medium heat in a large oven-proof skillet. Add onions and cook until soft, about 3 minutes. Add cumin, and cook until fragrant, about 1 minute more.

4. Add fennel, raisins and chicken broth to the pan, and season with salt and pepper. Cover and cook in a 350°F oven for 20 minutes, or until fennel is tender.

5. Serve with roast meat, chicken, fish, or vegetarian pasta.

POTATO FENNEL "RISOTTO"

Risotto is usually prepared with rice, but this variation uses potatoes instead.

2 Tbs butter	¼ cup wine
1 Tbs olive oil	1 quart chicken stock
½ cup diced fennel	2 Tbs Parmesan cheese, grated
½ cup diced onion	salt, pepper and lemon juice to taste
2 cups peeled (opt) and diced potatoes	

1. Melt 1 Tbs butter and olive oil in a large sauce pan. Add fennel, onion and potato. Season with salt and pepper. Cook for 2 minutes, stirring every so often.

2. Add white wine and stir.

3. Add chicken stock, ½ cup at a time, stirring regularly.

4. Cook for 10 minutes, or until potatoes are tender.

5. Stir in remaining butter and Parmesan. Adjust seasoning with salt, pepper and lemon juice.

PROSCIUTTO-WRAPPED GRILLED FIGS WITH BLUE CHEESE AND BALSAMIC

8 figs

1 tsp fresh thyme

8 slices prosciutto

2 cups balsamic vinegar

¼ cup white wine

1 shallot, diced

3 ounces Roquefort or other blue cheese

2 Tbs butter

OPTIONAL: arugula salad

1. Slice figs in half. Sprinkle with thyme. Wrap in prosciutto and secure with a toothpick.

2. Put 2 cups of balsamic vinegar in a pot, reduce over high heat until about ½ cup remains and the balsamic is syrupy. Remove from heat.

3. In medium sauce pan, add white wine and shallots. Reduce over high heat until only 2 Tbs of liquid remain. Reduce heat to low (or turn heat off completely), and vigorously whisk in cheese and 2 Tbs of whole butter. Set aside in warm place (does not reheat well).

4. Grill figs until prosciutto is slightly charred and figs are heated through. (Alternatively, set under the broiler for a few minutes). Serve with blue cheese and the balsamic glaze.

5. Garnish with an arugula salad, if you'd like.

GARLIC SCAPE VICHYSSOISE

3 Tbs butter

12 garlic scapes, coarsely chopped

1 leek, white and light green, chopped and then washed

½ cup white wine

1 pound potatoes, peeled and diced

6 cups water

¼ cup cream

salt and pepper to taste

more scapes, scallions or chives, chopped, for garnish

1. Heat pot over medium heat. Add butter. Add scapes and leeks. Cook for about 5 minutes, or until soft. Deglaze with white wine. Cook for 5 minutes more, or until the pan is mostly dry again (about 1 Tbs of liquid remains).

2. Add potatoes and water. Season with salt and pepper. Simmer for about 30 minutes, or until potatoes are tender.

3. Purée soup in a food processor. Add cream. Adjust seasoning with salt and (white) pepper.

4. Chill soup before serving. Garnish with scapes.

ARUGULA SOUFFLÉ

This recipe is adapted from the Silver Palate Cookbook. *It makes an elegant start to an early spring dinner.*

3 Tbs butter, plus extra for buttering the soufflé dish

4 Tbs flour

1 ½ cups half –n- half

6 eggs separated + 2 egg whites (for a total of 6 yolks and 8 whites)

4 bunches arugula (about 3 – 4 cups), washed and tougher stems removed

4 ounces soft goat cheese

pinch cayenne pepper

pinch nutmeg

⅛ tsp cream of tartar

salt and pepper to taste

1. Preheat the oven to 375°F. Butter a 2-quart soufflé dish.

2. Make the soufflé base: Melt the butter in a medium sauce pan over medium heat. Add the flour and cook, stirring constantly until the butter starts to foam. While still on the heat, slowly whisk in the half-n-half. Remove from heat, and whisk in the egg yolks.

3. Finely chop the arugula in a food processor, or by hand. Mix into the soufflé base, along with the goat cheese. Season with cayenne, nutmeg, salt and pepper.

4. Combine the egg whites, a pinch of salt and the cream of tartar in a bowl. Whisk at a high speed (with an electric mixer) until the whites are stiff.

5. Gently fold egg whites into soufflé base. Pour into soufflé dish and bake for 35-45 minutes, or until well puffed and golden. The center be just firm or have the slightest bit of wiggle.

6. Serve immediately.

ROASTED PEARS WITH ARUGULA AND PROSCIUTTO

2 Bosc pears

2 Tbs balsamic vinegar

1 Tbs fresh chopped thyme

2 Tbs butter

2 bunches arugula

2 Tbs extra virgin olive oil 1 lemon, juiced

6 slices prosciutto

¼ cup fresh shaved Parmesan

salt and pepper to taste

1. Peel pears. Slice in half, and scoop out core. Season with balsamic, thyme, salt and pepper. Put in a roasting pan, add butter and bake at 425°F for 15 minutes, or until soft.

2. Toss arugula with olive oil, then with lemon juice. Season to taste with salt and pepper. Divide arugula into 6 bundles and wrap each bundle with a prosciutto slice.

3. When pears are cooked, slice thinly. Drape over arugula-bundles. Sprinkle Parmesan on top.

GINGER SESAME BOK CHOY

This recipe works well with Tat Soi, Swiss chard and/or Napa Cabbage though the greens should be cut into 1-inch pieces instead of being left whole.

3 large or 6 small heads bok choy

2 Tbs dark roasted sesame oil (such as Kadoya brand)

3 cloves garlic, peeled and chopped

1 tsp fresh ginger, minced

¼ tsp black pepper, or to taste

¼ cup sake or white wine

2 Tbs mild soy sauce or 1 Tbs double dark soy sauce

2 Tbs butter

salt and lemon juice, to taste

1. Cut whole heads longitudinally in half and rinse thoroughly.

2. In a large skillet, heat sesame oil over medium heat. Add garlic and ginger, sauté for 2 minutes, or until garlic just begins to soften. Add bok choy halves, cut side down, and pepper.

3. Cover the greens and steam for 1 minute. Add sake or white wine and soy sauce. Flip bok choy.

4. When inner core is just soft (about 3 minutes, depending on size), add butter. Shake pan to incorporate.

5. Adjust seasoning with salt and lemon juice if necessary.

BRAISED ENDIVE WITH WATERCRESS AND APPLE SALAD

2 large endive, cut in half lengthwise, or 4 small endive

2 Tbs sugar

2 lemons, juiced

¾ cup grated Gruyere or Swiss cheese

1 red apple

1 bunch watercress

1 shallot, diced

1 Tbs cider vinegar

3 Tbs extra virgin olive oil

salt and pepper to taste

1. Put endive in pot with sugar and lemon juice. Cover with water. Season water to taste with salt and pepper, and additional lemon juice or sugar as necessary. Bring water to a boil, reduce heat to simmer. Let endive simmer for 30 minutes, or until tender.

2. When the endive are tender, remove from liquid. Put endive in an oven-proof dish. Cover with cheese. Melt cheese in oven (350°F) for 5 minutes.

3. Meanwhile, core and slice apple thinly (do not peel). Toss apples and watercress with vinegar, olive oil and shallots. Season to taste with salt and pepper (and fresh thyme if you'd like).

4. Serve half a large endive or 1 whole small endive per person with a small watercress and apple salad.

TAILLEVENT'S CREAM OF CRESS SOUP WITH CAVIAR

Patricia Wells describes Taillevent Restaurant in Paris as "a place that my husband, Walter, and we reserve for special occasions." And she describes its watercress soup as "the perfect choice for a celebratory New Year's Eve dinner. Like so much of the fare at this august restaurant, this soup shines with simple elegance."

The recipe is a lot of work and is absolutely worth it. This is one of the finest soups we've ever eaten, and 90% of non-caviar lovers have added caviar to their second serving. It is adapted from National Public Radio.

THE LEEK AND STOCK BASE:
- 3 Tbs unsalted butter
- 1 pound leeks, white and tender green portions, rinsed, halved, and thinly sliced
- 1 onion, peeled and finely chopped
- sea salt
- 1 quart homemade chicken stock
- 2 cup heavy cream (or whole milk)

THE CRESS:
- 3 Tbs sea salt
- 1 gallon English cress or curly American mustard, or 4 bunches watercress, roots and stems removed; washed

THE CREAM:
- 1 cup heavy cream
- juice of 1 lemon
- sea salt
- freshly ground white pepper (or black pepper, but this will leave flecks in an otherwise pure white cream)
- 2 Tbs caviar; lumpfish works and is more ecologically defensible than sturgeon.

1. In a 6-quart stock-pot, combine the butter, leeks, onions, and a pinch of sea salt. Cook, covered and over low heat, until soft but not browned, about 3 minutes. Add the chicken stock and cream. Simmer gently, uncovered, for 30 minutes.

2. Purée the soup in a blender, food processor, or with a handheld immersion blender until emulsified into a smooth-textured mixture.

3. Return the mixture to the saucepan, increase the heat to high, and bring to a gentle boil. Using a slotted spoon, skim off any impurities that may rise to the surface. Set this base aside. (This mixture can be prepared up to 1 day in advance. To store, cover and refrigerate.)

4. Prepare a large bowl full of ice water.

5. In a 6-quart pasta pot fitted with a colander, bring 4 quarts water to a boil over high heat. Add the sea salt and the greens. Blanch, uncovered, until soft and wilted, 2 to 3 minutes. Immediately remove the colander

from the water, drain the cress, and plunge the colander into the ice water to stop the cooking. Drain again, and purée the cress in a food processor. Place the purée in a fine-mesh sieve, and carefully press out (and discard) any remaining liquid. Set the purée aside.

6. In the bowl of a heavy-duty mixer fitted with a whisk (or with a handheld mixer), whip the cream at high speed until stiff. Add the lemon juice, and season to taste with sea salt and white pepper. Set aside.

7. At serving time, reheat the soup base until simmering. Remove it from the heat and add the cress purée, stirring until thoroughly blended. Serve the soup in warm, shallow soup bowls, placing a scoop of the whipped cream in the center of each bowl. Top with a small spoonful of caviar, and serve.

6 servings

WARM FRISÉE AND SPINACH SALAD WITH MUSTARD VINAIGRETTE

VINAIGRETTE
- 2 tsp Dijon mustard
- 2 tsp red wine vinegar
- 2 ½ Tbs extra virgin olive oil
- ½ tsp fresh thyme
- salt and pepper to taste

SALAD
- 2 slices bacon or 2 Tbs olive oil
- 1 small red onion, peeled and thinly sliced
- 1 bunch frisée
- ¼ pound baby spinach

1. Combine mustard and vinegar in a bowl. Whisk in olive oil. Season with thyme, salt and pepper.

2. Cut bacon into cubes. Cook in skillet over medium flame until it is just starting to brown (but not fully crispy). If using olive oil, heat over medium heat.

3. Add onions, turn heat to high and continue cooking for 3 minutes or until bacon and onions are crisp.

4. Drain excess fat from bacon, and toss warm bacon over greens.

5. Dress salad with the vinaigrette. Season to taste with salt and pepper.

BASIC ITALIAN SAUTÉED GREENS

1 large bunch of pre-washed kale, collards, or mustard greens

¾-inch water to steam or 2 quarts salted water to boil

ice bath (see "Shocking" section in the Key Techniques chapter)

1 ½ tsp olive oil + 1½ tsp neutral oil

2 – 4 cloves garlic, coarsely chopped

salt and pepper to taste

1. Barely wilt greens in steamer or by blanching; shock in ice bath if you'll not immediately sauté. Drain. Coarsely chop.

2. Sauté greens by heating garlic in oils until garlic edges have just started to brown, and IMMEDIATELY dump drained greens into the skillet. Stir around and sauté about 30 more seconds. Will cool quickly, so a lidded serving dish is apt.

VARIATIONS OF THE BASIC ITALIAN:

a) Delete the garlic, and substitute for it slivered onions, half-moons of yellow summer squash or zucchini, and/or sweet red pepper pieces.

b) Keep garlic and onions, and add 1 Tbs butter or ½ cup heavy cream to the skillet when the greens are almost done. Serve with toasted chopped almonds, or whole toasted pine nuts, on top.

c) Add fresh sage or rosemary to the hot skillet the second before adding the greens.

BASIC CHINESE SAUTÉED GREENS

Use the exact same ingredients as the basic Italian, but exchange the olive oil with toasted sesame oil (e.g., Kadoya), substitute 1 Tbs soy sauce for the last salt, and sauté 1 tsp fresh minced ginger with the garlic. Proceed as per the basic Italian.

VARIATIONS OF THE BASIC CHINESE:

a) Add more vegetables, especially 1½-inch pieces of scallion, sliced Brussels sprouts, sweet red pepper, etc.

b) Add pre-cooked, drained udon, Asian vermicelli, or ramen noodles to the skillet when the greens are nearly done. Increase seasoning appropriately.

c) Add 2-3 beaten eggs to the sautéing greens; cook to scramble. Serve over steamed rice and re-season. Excellent boost for people just recovering from sickness.

CREAMED BRAISING GREENS

This recipe comes courtesy of longtime Even' Star friend and CSA subscriber Sherry Jones.

6 Tbs butter

2 cloves garlic, minced

1 shallot, peeled and thinly sliced

1 cup heavy cream

pinch freshly grated nutmeg

salt

3-4 pounds young greens, like collards, kale or mustard – stemmed and finely shredded (chiffonade)

1. In a saucepan, heat 2 Tablespoons of the butter over high heat until it foams. Add the garlic and shallot and cook over medium-low heat, stirring, until softened and golden, 5 minutes. Add the cream, bring to a simmer and cook until slightly thickened, 10 minutes. Add the nutmeg and salt to taste. Using a hand blender, puree until smooth.

2. In a large pot, heat the remaining 4 Tablespoons of butter over high heat until it foams. Add the greens and cook, stirring constantly, until tender but still bright green, about 5 minutes. Sprinkle with salt and add the cream mixture. Lower the heat, cover and let simmer until cooked through, 5 minutes more. Taste for nutmeg and salt, season to taste and serve hot.

Yield: 8 servings

KALE CHIPS

Kale chips are surprisingly light and delicate and not at all greasy. They couldn't be more simple to make.

1 pound kale, cored, leaves rinsed and thoroughly dried

3-4 Tbs olive oil

salt and pepper, to taste

1. Toss kale leaves in olive oil, salt and pepper.

2. Spread them out on a single layer and bake at 250°F for 20 to 30 minutes, until crispy.

3. Left-overs can be stored in an air-tight container at room temperature.

BUTTON MUSHROOMS AND GREENS

This is excellent served with crusty bread, freshly boiled potatoes or baked potatoes. It is also lovely served over pasta or alongside chicken or scallops. Generous addition of freshly ground black pepper can really highlight all the flavors.

1 large bunch pre-washed greens: kale, collards, mustard greens or Swiss chard

2 tsp olive oil

½ onion, sliced

2 cloves garlic

1 pint button mushrooms (portobellos or crimini would also work well), sliced ¼-inch thick

¼ cup white wine

1 tsp salt, plus salt and pepper to taste

1 ½ cup heavy cream

1. Pre-blanch and shock the greens: in a large pot of boiling, salted water, cook greens until just wilted, approximately for 1 minute and drain. Shock in an ice bath, and drain well.

2. Coarsely chop greens if desired, or leave whole.

3. In a large skillet, add oil. Over medium-high heat, cook onions and garlic until barely translucent. Add the mushrooms and continue cooking for 1 minute more, stirring often.

4. Add white wine to mushroom pan and simmer for 2 minutes.

5. Add cream and continue cooking to reduce for 5 more minutes, until approximately 1 cup of liquid remains.

6. Add the greens, stir well, adjust seasoning with salt and freshly ground black pepper. Cook only until greens are heated through, about 30 seconds.

CHICK PEA CREPES STUFFED WITH WILTED GREENS

This recipe was inspired by the Southern France street-food – socca. A chick pea crepe baked in a cast-iron skillet.

½ cups chick-pea flour
¼ cup all-purpose flour
1 egg yolk
¾ cup water (or a mix of cream and water)
1 Tbs extra virgin olive oil, plus extra for cooking

1 bunch kale or arugula, washed and coarsely chopped
2 cloves garlic, chopped
2 Tbs pine nuts
2 Tbs currants or raisins
¼ tsp curry powder

1. Sift flours with salt and pepper. Make a well in the center. Add the egg and water. Whisk to incorporate. Add the olive oil. The batter should be the consistency of heavy cream. Let rest for 30 minutes.

2. Meanwhile, heat a large skillet over medium heat. Add olive oil, raisins and garlic. When garlic starts to brown add the curry powder and pine nuts. Cook for 1 minute more and add the greens. Cook until just wilted. Coarsely chop the greens. Season with salt and pepper.

3. Heat a non-stick skillet over medium heat. Brush the bottom of the pan with olive oil. Pour in a thin layer of batter, and cook until set. Flip over and cook for 30 seconds more. Remove from pan and repeat process until all the crepes are made.

4. Roll each crepe like a cigar with about ½ cup of filling. Reheat just before serving, and slice in half.

CLASSIC ITALIAN GREENS AND GARLIC SOUP

Working outside in the winter for his living has taught Brett the value of great simple soups on frigid days. This one works best with homemade chicken or turkey broth, but vegetarian or purchased stocks can also do nicely.

3 cloves garlic, chopped

1 tsp olive oil

¼ cup white wine

1 quart good poultry or vegetarian broth

tortellini, ravioli, capellini, egg noodles, etc.

½ tsp black pepper

½ – 1 tsp salt 1 large bunch pre-

washed cooking greens (such as kale, collards, arugula Swiss chard or bok choy), coarsely chopped

1 tsp (per diner) pesto or chopped fresh basil (optional)

1 baguette or similar crusty bread

1 bottle good to very good wine, red or white

1. In a large pot, sauté garlic in olive oil until soft; immediately add ¼ cup white wine. Add broth and bring to boil. Add pasta of your choosing, continue boiling until pasta is just cooked, remove pot from heat, taste and adjust seasoning. (If meal will be delayed, remove pasta immediately with a slotted spoon. It easily overcooks.) Stir in greens and immediately serve.

2. The good bread really complements the dish, as does the basil, stirred in by each diner. Commercial pesto is easier to get in the depths of winter than is fresh or frozen basil. This recipe on its own justifies having a stock of basil in oil in your freezer, prepped during the glory days of summer.

3. The wine is for you to drink, especially if you needn't return to work.

CLASSIC SOUTHERN-STYLE GREENS

This staple of the American South is still great comfort food. We advise seeking out the absolute best bacon or ham you can find; most commercial types such as Smithfield and Armour have lots of water and chemicals added.

¼ – ½ pound bacon, ham, or sausage, raw but coarsely chopped
1 onion, sliced or chopped
1 large bunch pre-washed collards, kale, mustards, etc., coarsely chopped

½ tsp black pepper
salt only after tasting

1. Bake meat in heavy skillet at 350°F until crisping at edges. Pour off most of fat but retain at least 2 Tbs. Add onion and continue baking until onions and meat are fully cooked, about 15 minutes.

2. Carefully remove from oven, add greens, and sauté on the stove-top until greens are just wilted or beyond. Season with salt tot taste. May also add a touch of vinegar.

Nice served with sweet potato, herbed grits, or mashed potato. The first time we were served this dish properly prepared, we were encouraged to join our hosts in bourbon and soda, and that beverage still fits.

KOSHER EQUIVALENT TO THE SOUTHERN-STYLE GREENS

A worthy take on the above deletes the pork, and substitutes ground beef; coarsely chopped, cooked brisket; or boneless skin-on, coarsely chopped chicken thigh meat (breast meat won't do it justice: it is too dry). All other procedures and ingredients are the same. The chicken lightens the dish considerably relative to the pork or beef.

VEGETARIAN EQUIVALENT TO THE SOUTHERN-STYLE GREENS

The basic Southern-style is even fit for a meatless approach. Sauté 2 sliced onions in 2 Tbs oil under moderate flame until fully caramelized (browning at edges, or more); add 1 Tbs soy sauce, and then proceed as per the above. Particularly nice with fresh thyme added late, or fresh basil added after the cooking is all done.

WARM SALAD SPIN-OFF OF SOUTHERN-STYLE GREENS

Use only the most tender of cooking greens, and let the out-of-the-oven skillet cool a bit more for this variation. Barely wilt the greens (about 5 seconds) in the skillet and immediately transfer to a cool serving dish. Splash 1 tsp red wine or cider vinegar into the skillet, loosen all the caramelized bits, and drizzle all over the greens. Particularly nice on blustery winter nights.

COCONUT CURRIED VEGETABLES

We prefer sweet potatoes, kale and tomatoes in this recipe for the flavor, color and textural contrasts, but you could use any veggies you like.

1 Tbs plain oil

2 garlic cloves, chopped

½ onion, chopped

1 Tbs Chinese chili-garlic paste (more or less to taste)

1 sweet potato, peeled and cubed into ¾–inch pieces

1 13-ounce can coconut milk

1 bunch kale, washed and coarsely chopped

2 plum tomatoes, chopped

1 Tbs fried shallots or onions*

Salt or fish sauce to taste

1. In a large skillet, heat oil over medium high heat. Add garlic and onions and cook until they wilt and start to brown.

2. Add the chili paste and sweet potatoes and stir to evenly mix everything. Cook for 2 minutes to toast the chili paste and bring out its flavor.

3. Add the coconut milk and reduce heat to simmer. Season with salt or fish sauce. Cook, covered, until the sweet potatoes are just tender, about 15 minutes.

4. Add the kale and tomatoes and cook until the kale is wilted and tender, about 5 minutes more.

5. Sprinkle fried shallots on top. Serve over steamed rice.

*Fried shallots can be purchased at Asian supermarkets. Or you can make your own by frying thin slices of peeled shallots in plenty of canola oil over medium heat for 12 - 15 minutes, or until golden brown. Drain on a paper towel. Oil can be reserved for other cooking uses.

KALE SAUTÉED WITH BACON, SCAPES AND LEMON

Swiss Chard would also work well.

2 slices bacon, diced	¼ tsp chili flakes (optional)
½ pound kale, coarsely chopped	Juice of ½ lemon
2 – 3 garlic scapes, chopped	salt and pepper to taste

1. Heat a large a large skillet. Add the bacon and cook until the fat starts to render, and the bacon begins to brown. Drain off excess fat.

2. To the bacon pan, add the scapes and chili flakes, and then the kale. Cook for 3 minutes, or until kale is wilted and tender.

3. Season to taste with salt and pepper. Squeeze lemon on top just before serving.

REFRESHING RAW KALE SALAD WITH SESAME SEEDS

1 gallon kale, washed
¼ cup sesame seeds
½ cup pepita or hulled sunflower seeds
1 small red onion

¼ cup lemon juice
¼ cup soy sauce
¼ cup olive oil
black pepper

1. Remove stems/ribs from kale. Cut into thin strips. Put into a large salad bowl.

2. In a small skillet, attentively toast the sesame and pepita seeds over medium heat, stirring frequently. When the sesame seeds begin to turn golden remove from heat and set aside.

3. Peel the onion and slice as thin as possible.

4. Mix the dressing: combine the soy sauce, lemon juice and olive oil.

5. Toss the kale with the seeds, dressing and onions. Let sit for at least one hour, mixing occasionally.

6. Season with black pepper to taste.

SAVORY VEGETARIAN GREENS AND POTATOES

3 – 4 average sized russet potatoes, washed but with skins on

1 large bunch any cooking greens – kale, collards, Swiss chard, or even arugula

3 – 6 Tbs mix of olive and neutral oils

3 cloves garlic, chopped

1 large onion, chopped

1 tsp black pepper

½ – 1 tsp salt

½ bunch scallions

fresh basil, or 1 tsp dried oregano, basil, or rosemary

salt and pepper to taste

1. Dice potatoes to yield about 3 cups. Toss with about ½ tsp of salt and let sit for about 5 minutes.

2. Coarsely chop the greens

3. In a heavy skillet (works best in seasoned cast iron), sauté the potatoes for about 5 minutes, or until they start to brown. Add the onion and garlic and continue cooking until barely soft. Add the greens, and cook two minutes more or until they are wilted. Stir in the herbs and chopped scallion. If needed, season further before serving: this should be hearty, not bland.

4. Can nicely be served with a dollop of sour cream, home-made guacamole, or with grated cheddar or Monterey jack on top. Also really good with 1 tsp whole cumin seed (added to skillet right before spuds go in) in lieu of or in addition to other herbs. Hot peppers complement the latter approach well.

CURRIED GREENS

2 tsp vegetable oil
1 onion, chopped
1 clove garlic, chopped
¼ tsp whole cumin seed
½ – 1 tsp curry powder

1 large bunch pre-washed cooking greens
salt and pepper to taste
¼ cup plain yogurt (optional)

1. Sauté onions, cumin seed and curry powder together in oil until the onions are translucent, then add greens to cook until just wilted or beyond. Add yogurt if desired and reduce heat.

2. Nice served alongside brown or Basmati rice, or with pan-fried potatoes.

CURRIED GREENS STUFFING FOR CHICKEN

2 Tbs butter
3 cloves garlic, sliced
1 ½ tsp curry powder
1 bunch mustard greens or other pre-washed cooking greens, coarsely chopped

½ cup raisins
salt and pepper to taste

1. Melt butter in sauté pan. Add garlic. Cook for 2 minutes over medium heat, and add the curry powder. Cook for 1 more minute and add the raisins.

2. Add the mustard greens, and cook until they wilt.

3. Cool before using stuffing. Stuff under skin of chicken breast before baking.

BABY SPINACH SALAD WITH A WARM SHERRY VINAIGRETTE AND DRIED CHERRIES

½ cup extra virgin olive oil	1 Tbs fresh lemon juice
1 shallot or small onion, sliced	2 Tbs sherry or malt vinegar
1 Tbs chopped thyme	1 pound baby spinach
2 cloves garlic, chopped	croutons
¼ cup dried cherries or cranberries	salt and pepper to taste

1. Make the vinaigrette, heat olive oil in a pan over low heat. Add shallots, and cook until they begin to wilt, about 3 minutes. Add garlic, thyme and dried cherries. Cook for 1 minute more. Add lemon juice and vinegar.

2. Put spinach in a bowl. Toss with warm dressing. Garnish salad with croutons. Serve immediately.

CHILLED SPINACH SALAD WITH SESAME DRESSING

This recipe is inspired by the traditional Japanese dish, Gomae Spinach.

1 pound fresh spinach, washed	2 Tbs soy sauce
8 Tbs roasted sesame seeds	1 Tbs rice vinegar
2 Tbs sake or dry sherry	¼ cup water or dashi
2 tsp sugar	

1. Heat a large skillet over high flame. Add spinach (no oil, just the residual water from washing). Cook the spinach just until it wilts, turning occasionally.

2. Chill spinach in refrigerator.

3. Meanwhile, in a food processor, combine the remaining ingredients together. Blend until smooth, approximately 3 minutes.

4. Squeeze out excess water from spinach. Drizzle dressing on top just before serving.

CREAMED SPINACH

¼ cup white wine
1 small shallot or onion, diced
2 garlic cloves, sliced
1 cup cream

2 large bunches of spinach, washed, stemmed and coarsely chopped (or 1 pound baby spinach)
salt and pepper to taste

1. In a large sauté pan, reduce wine with shallot and garlic until there is almost no liquid.

2. Add the cream, and reduce the cream until it is very thick and about ¼ cup remains. Do not worry that it will be too thick as the liquid from the spinach will thin it.

3. Add spinach. Cook until it wilts. Season with salt, pepper and lemon juice.

KOREAN-STYLE SPINACH SALAD

1 pound spinach, washed
2 Tbs soy sauce
½ Tbs sugar
1 Tbs rice vinegar

1 Tbs scallion
½ Tbs ground sesame seeds
OPTIONAL: ½ tsp chopped garlic)

1. Heat a large skillet over high flame. Add spinach (no oil, just the residual water from washing). Cook the spinach just until it wilts, turning occasionally. Remove from pan and let cool.

2. Mix remaining ingredients together and toss with spinach.

SWISS CHARD QUICHE

1 home-made or frozen pie crust, zero sugar if possible

1 large bunch Swiss chard

salted water to blanch

1 tsp olive oil

1 medium onion, chopped

2 Tbs white wine

2 cups milk, half –n- half, or light cream

3 large eggs (or 4 medium)

2 Tbs chopped fresh herbs such as chervil, parsley, dill, tarragon, or thyme, or dry if need be (1 tsp)

¼ – ½ pound Gruyere, Cheddar, jack, mozzarella, or similar cheese, grated

1 tsp salt

½ tsp black pepper

OPTIONAL: pine nuts, almonds, garlic and fresh basil.

1. If making your own crust, consider adding ½ tsp dried thyme to the flour before cutting in the shortening. Pre-bake crust until barely brown at edges. Keep oven at 350°F.

2. Meanwhile, blanch or steam the greens, shock, drain as thoroughly as possible, and chop medium or coarsely. Set aside. Sauté onion in olive oil until translucent, add white wine, and simmer 1 more minute. Let cool.

3. Make batter by beating together milk, eggs, salt and pepper, herbs, and onion-wine mix.

4. Place drained chopped greens into pie shell. Sprinkle grated cheese over greens, then pour batter over all. Bake about 50 minutes, until center of quiche doesn't jiggle when you poke the pie pan's edge. Center of quiche should also be slightly raised and golden brown at this point. Remove from oven and let cool at least 10 and as many as 60 minutes before serving. This gives clean edges to crust and filling upon cutting and plating.

5. For a particularly Italianate variant of this, add 3 cloves garlic to the sautéing onions, use dry or fresh basil in lieu of other herbs, and sprinkle pine nuts atop the cheese before pouring in the batter.

SWISS CHARD AND RICOTTA DUMPLINGS

These dumplings can be made a day in advance, up to step 6, and heated with the melted butter or sauce and cheese before serving.

1 pound Swiss chard or spinach to make 1 ⅓ cups squeezed cooked greens
1 Tbs olive oil
2 – 3 chopped garlic cloves
1 cup ricotta, drained in a sieve if watery
½ cup grated Parmesan
2 eggs
½ cup flour

1 lemon, zested
pinch of nutmeg
salt and pepper to taste

FOR THE SAUCE:
¼ cup melted butter, ½ cup tomato sauce (mixed with pine nuts and raisins), or ½ cup homemade tomato-meat sauce
¼ cup grated Parmesan

1. Wash the greens in a sinkful of warm water to clean. Dirty spinach may need more than one change of water. Lift the greens from the water and drain them in a colander. Remove any thick stems.

2. Heat a large skillet over high heat. Add olive oil and garlic. When garlic becomes fragrant, add greens. Cook for 3-5 minutes or until bright green and wilted. Remove the greens and place them in a colander. Let cool.

3. Divide the greens in three parts and squeeze to remove all excess water. Reserve the liquid to add to sauce.

4. Coarsely chop the greens with a knife and then put in the food processor. Add the ricotta, Parmesan, egg, 1 tsp salt, lemon zest and nutmeg. Process to form a smooth paste. Fold in flour.

5. Bring a large pot of water to a boil. Season generously with salt. Transfer the paste to a pastry bag with a large tip or a medium-sized plastic bag with a ½-inch corner cut off. Pipe out ½-inch dumplings. Alternatively, use two spoons to form dumplings and drop into water.

6. Poach 8-9 dumplings at a time, for 2-3 minutes or until they float to the surface of the water. Transfer with a slotted spoon to a large baking dish.

7. Preheat the oven to 400°F. Drizzle the dumpling with melted butter, or tomato or meat sauce, and sprinkle with grated cheese. Bake for 10-15 minutes or until lightly browned and cheese has melted and serve.

GINGER SAUTÉED TAT SOI WITH TOFU

6 ounces extra firm tofu, sliced
½-inch thick

2 Tbs soy sauce

¼ tsp rice vinegar

2 tsp brown sugar

2 tsp lime juice

1 Tbs canola oil

1 – 2 tsp toasted sesame seeds

2 tsp fresh ginger, minced

1 tsp garlic, minced

¼ tsp chili flakes

2 small bunches of tat soi or bok choy

1 tsp sesame oil

1. Put tofu slices on a paper towel to dry them.

2. In a small bowl, combine the soy sauce, vinegar, sugar and lime juice.

3. In a large skillet (preferably non-stick) over medium-high heat, add canola oil and a few drops of the sesame oil. Add tofu slices; cook for 5-7 minutes per side, or until golden brown. Remove from skillet. Add remaining sesame oil to skillet. Add ginger and garlic and cook for 1 minute, or until fragrant. Add the chili flakes and then the tat soi, and stir for a minute more. When the tat soi starts to wilt, add the sauce and cook for 3 minutes more, or until sauce begins to thicken.

4. Divide greens on plates. Top with half of the tofu. Drizzle with remaining sauce, and sprinkle with sesame seeds. Serve immediately.

WHITE BEAN AND GREENS SOUP WITH CHICKEN SAUSAGE

2 Tbs olive oil

1 onion, coarsely chopped

4 garlic cloves, coarsely chopped

½ celery stalk, coarsely chopped

1 large carrot, peeled and coarsely chopped

2 cups cooked white beans

5 cups chicken broth, water, or combination of the two

1 piece of Parmesan rind

1 sprig fresh thyme, chopped

½ pound smoked chicken sausage, sliced

1 pound turnip greens, kale, Swiss chard or collards, coarsely chopped

2 tsp salt

½ tsp black pepper

1. Heat oil in a large pot over medium heat. Add onions, garlic, celery and carrots, and cook until soft, about 4 or 5 minutes. Add beans, liquid, cheese rind, and thyme. Season to taste with salt and pepper. Bring to a boil and reduce to a simmer. Cook uncovered for about 20 minutes.

2. Meanwhile, brown sausage in batches over medium heat. Cut into chunks.

3. Stir greens and sausage into soup. Cook for 2-5 minutes or until greens are wilted and tender.

4. Add water, if necessary to thin soup. Adjust seasoning with salt and pepper to taste.

POTATO AND JERUSALEM ARTICHOKE GRATIN

This is a rich casserole that can serve as a whole meal if served with a good salad. No need to use fresh new potatoes; anything will do.

2 Tbs butter	chopped
2 pounds potatoes, washed, not peeled, but sliced very thin	2 tsp salt
	¾ tsp black pepper
1 pound Jerusalem artichokes, not peeled, scrubbed and sliced very thin	1 onion, chopped
	½ cup grated cheese: cheddar, Gouda, Gruyere or Parmesan
2 cup milk, half -n- half, or cream	OPTIONAL: 1 pint arugula, chopped, and/or 1 apple, chopped
5 medium-large cloves garlic,	

1. Butter a 9-inch x 13-inch Pyrex dish.

2. In a large bowl, mix all ingredients together (including optionals) and then place into the baking dish. With the back of a spatula, press down the potatoes and Jerusalem artichokes so they lay flat and are submerged in the cream.

3. Bake at 340°F until tender all the way through, about 40 minutes. Test by inserting a butter knife into the middle of the dish. If it goes in easily, the potatoes are cooked.

4. Let cool for 10 minutes before slicing and serving.

ROASTED JERUSALEM ARTICHOKES WITH SAGE

1 pound Jerusalem artichokes
2 Tbs olive oil
3 cloves garlic, chopped
2 – 3 Tbs fresh sage, thinly sliced

2 Tbs butter
salt, pepper and lemon juice, to taste

1. Scrub and wash well Jerusalem artichokes (but do not peel) and cut into ¼-inch chunks. Toss with olive oil and season with salt and pepper.

2. Put Jerusalem artichokes on a baking sheet or Pyrex dish. Roast at 375°F for 10 minutes.

3. Remove pan from oven and stir in garlic, sage and butter. Continue baking for an additional 10 minutes more or until artichokes are tender and garlic is lightly golden.

4. Squeeze lemon juice on top just before serving.

KOHLRABI AND APPLE SLAW

This recipe scales up or down very easily. The important factor is to have equal parts of kohlrabi and apple.

1 – 2 kohlrabi

1 – 2 red crisp or snacking apples, such as gala or honey crisp

fresh herbs, such as basil, tarragon, mint and/or parsley, chopped

DRESSING

¼ cup mayonnaise

1 Tbs sour cream or plain yogurt

1 Tbs lemon juice

½ Tbs Dijon mustard

½ tsp sugar

salt and pepper to taste

1. Combine ingredients for the dressing.

2. Peel kohlrabi and cut into small matchsticks.

3. Core apple (but do not peel: the skin adds a nice texture, color and flavor). Cut into matchsticks.

4. Toss kohlrabi with apples, dressing and fresh herbs.

KOHLRABI SALAD

When visiting Vietnam a few years ago, Julia noticed many chefs using kohlrabi in place of green papaya for their crisp salads. This recipe follows that trend.

2 kohlrabi	1 lime, juiced
2 shallots or 1 red onion, chopped	3 Tbs fish sauce
3 – 4 chilies	2 tomatoes, diced
4 garlic cloves	6 green beans, cut into thin strips
½ tsp salt	2 Tbs unsalted, roasted peanuts
1 Tbs sugar	

1. Peel kohlrabi. Slice very thin, or shred with a mandolin.

2. With a mortar and pestle (or in a food processor), grind the shallots, salt, half the chilies and garlic.

3. Toss kohlrabi with garlic paste. Season with sugar, lime juice and fish sauce.

4. Toss with beans and tomatoes.

5. Garnish with peanuts.

ROASTED KOHLRABI

1 ½ pounds kohlrabi, ends trimmed, thick green skin sliced off with a knife and diced

1 Tbs olive oil

1 Tbs garlic

2 slices raw bacon, chopped (optional)

1 – 2 Tbs red wine vinegar

salt

1. Preheat oven to 425°F.

2. Toss the diced kohlrabi with olive oil, garlic, bacon (if using) and salt in a bowl. Spread in a single layer on a rimmed baking sheet and put into oven (it needn't be fully preheated) and roast for 30 - 35 minutes; after 20 minutes, stir every five minutes.

3. Sprinkle with vinegar just before serving.

BRAISED LEEKS WITH MUSTARD VINAIGRETTE

1 Tbs butter

4 leeks, dark green tops removed, cut in half lengthwise and washed

1 sprig thyme

¼ cup white wine

1 cup chicken or vegetable broth

2 slices bacon, diced (or walnuts)

1 cup arugula

mustard vinaigrette

salt and black pepper

1. Melt butter in a skillet, add the leeks in a single layer, cut side down. Brown a little before adding a sprig of thyme and the wine. Let the wine reduce and then add the stock, salt and pepper to taste.

2. Put leeks in a 350°F oven for 20 minute to braise, or until softened. Set aside.

3. Put the diced bacon in a pan in the oven to render the fat and get crispy. Drain the bacon on a paper towel. If using walnuts, toast in the oven for 10 minutes or until they become fragrant.

4. To serve, dress the arugula in mustard vinaigrette and put on plate. Lay the leeks on the plate and sprinkle bacon bits or walnuts on top.

MUSTARD VINAIGRETTE

1 tsp whole grain mustard

2 tsp red wine vinegar

¼ cup extra virgin olive oil

salt and pepper to taste

Whisk everything together.

BUTTERED LEEKS

Leeks rarely get the proper showing they deserve. This simple recipe lets their sweet onion flavor shine.

3 large leeks	½ tsp salt
2 Tbs butter	1 Tbs fresh lemon juice

1. Trim the leeks: cut off the dark green and set aside for another use. Cut the leeks in half lengthwise, then into ½-inch slices. Soak in cold water to remove the dirt. Lift the leeks out of the water.

2. Heat a large skillet over medium heat. Add the butter and let it melt. Then add the leeks and salt. Cook, stirring occasionally, until the leeks are soft, about 15 minutes.

BASIC SAUTÉED SHIITAKE OR WILD MUSHROOMS

1 quart wild or shiitake mushrooms	1 tsp butter
1 Tbs olive oil	2 Tbs white wine, brandy, bourbon,
½ small onion, minced	sherry, or beer
1 clove garlic, minced	salt and pepper to taste

1. Wash the mushrooms by immersing the caps in water (see greens technique in chapter 4). Drain well. Cut into chunks.

2. Heat olive oil in a large skillet over high heat. Add mushrooms first, then onions and garlic. Add butter and season with salt, pepper and booze. Cook until mushrooms are just soft.

3. Excellent with poultry, fish, omelets and especially red meat.

CAPELLINI WITH CHANTERELLES, CREAM AND LOBSTER

Delectable, absolutely delectable. A wonderful dish for special romantic occasions. Superb served with Champagne and crusty bread. Serves 2.

1 Tbs butter

1 tsp canola oil

½ onion or shallot, peeled and finely diced

1 - 2 cloves garlic, chopped

1 pint chanterelle mushrooms, washed and sliced ¼-inch thick

½ tsp salt

¼ black pepper

¼ dry white wine or brandy

1 pint heavy cream

½ pound capellini or angel hair pasta

meat from 1 ¼ pound lobster or ½ pound peeled shrimp or ½ pound scallops

3 sprigs fresh thyme or ¼ tsp dried thyme

2 Tbs chopped parsley

salt and pepper

OPTIONAL: fresh lemon juice

1. In a heavy bottom-skillet or sauce pan, over moderate heat, melt butter with oil. Add the onion and garlic, and saute until just transparent. Add chanterelles and saute 2 - 3 minutes. Add white wine or brandy, simmer for another minute. Add cream and thyme, black pepper and salt. Reduce heat to low, and until liquid is reduced by half its volume.

2. Meanwhile, bring a large pot of salted water to a boil.

3. While cream is reducing, cook pasta in boiling water according to package directions.

4. When cream is reduced, add the seafood, and cook 30 seconds more. Add thyme and parsley.

5. Drain pasta and immediately tossed with cream/shellfish/chanterelle mix. Adjust seasoning to taste with salt, pepper and lemon juice.

EVEN' STAR GUMBO

A deeply flavored stew of summer vegetables that mandates okra, one of whose African names is "gumbo" and the seed of which was carried to this continent by the slaves. Once made, the thick base can be frozen, to be thawed in deep winter, and simmered with poultry, seafood, sausage, or with only vegetables.

3 Tbs canola or other neutral oil

4 cloves garlic, chopped

½ onion, chopped

2 mild green peppers, chopped

2 cups ripe or overripe tomatoes, puréed

4 cups water, chicken or vegetable stock

I pint okra, cut into ¼-inch rounds

2 tsp dried thyme or 1 ½ oregano

2 tsp gumbo file powder (optional, but very good)

2 Tbs flour

salt, pepper, and hot pepper to taste

chopped scallions or parsley as final garnish

THE OMNIVORE OPTIONS: shrimp, chicken, game, scallops, crab, oysters, andouille or other sausage, or pork chunks

THE VEGETARIAN OPTIONS: sweet corn kernels, tempeh, eggplant, vegetarian sausage, and/or fresh mushrooms

1. In 1 Tbs of the oil and in a large stainless or cast iron pot, sauté the garlic, onion, and peppers until soft.

2. Add the puréed tomatoes and water or stock; simmer 10 more minutes.

3. Add the okra, herbs, salt, and pepper. Simmer 2 more minutes, then taste and adjust seasonings to taste.

4. If you want a thicker gumbo, make a roux by cooking the remaining two Tbs oil with 2 Tbs flour in a separate pan on moderate heat, stirring all the time. One minute after it starts bubbling, add into the larger pot of gumbo, beating vigorously with a whisk to prevent lumps. Simmer another 5 minutes, and again adjust seasonings to taste. This base may be frozen or used immediately.

5. To complete the gumbo, add whatever omnivore or vegetarian options you want, but be sure to add long-cooking items like chicken or sausage way before foods like shrimp or scallops that need only the briefest of cooking. Simmer all together until the brief-cookers are just tender.

6. Gumbo is nearly always served with cooked white rice, a spoonful in the center of each diner's bowl. This may be the best and only use for a converted rice like Uncle Ben's. Alternately, a crusty French or Italian bread does well. Sprinkle each bowl with the chopped parsley or scallion

at table-side. Excellent with a chilled white wine, any beer except stout or porter, or even a red wine (Portuguese or Spanish) or a moderately chilled Pinot Noir.

OKRA FRITTERS

1 cup flour	1 tsp baking soda
½ cup cornmeal	2 tsp salt
¼ cup grated Parmesan	½ tsp cayenne
1 medium onion, peeled and diced	1 pound okra, trimmed and sliced
3 eggs, lightly beaten	thin, about ¼-inch
1 ¼ cup buttermilk	1 cup canola oil

1. Make a batter by mixing together flour, cornmeal, Parmesan, onions, eggs, buttermilk, baking soda, salt and cayenne. Mix in okra.

2. Heat a large skillet over medium-high heat. Spoon in 4 – 5 fritters (2-3 Tbs) at a time. Fry until golden brown on each side, about 3 minutes. Drain on paper towels. Keep in a warm place while cooking remaining fritters.

Excellent with Romesco (page 256), Dreamy Green Goddess (page 250) or Agrodolce (page 265)

REFRESHING CHILLED OKRA

An excellent light appetizer to serve guests or yourself, especially when the heat of summer makes heavier foods less appealing.

1 heaping pint fresh tender okra
ice water bath in a medium bowl
2 or 3 tsp of any good vinaigrette (any in this book are good options)

1. Bring a pot of salted water to a boil. Steam or boil the okra until the color just changes from bright green to darker green, about 3 minutes. Immediately drain the okra and quickly shock them by dumping into the ice water bath.

2. Swirl okra in bath until cold, and then drain again.

3. Place onto a serving platter or into a pretty bowl. Chill. Drizzle vinaigrette onto the okra about 5 to 20 minutes before serving.

SAUTÉED OKRA OR SUMMER SQUASH WITH TOMATO AND CORN

2 medium summer squash or ½ pound fresh okra
1 medium beefsteak tomato
1 small onion
2 cloves garlic

1 ear corn
1 ½ Tbs olive oil or butter
1 Tbs fresh Genoa basil
salt, pepper and lemon juice to taste

1. Cut squash or okra into ½-inch-thick slices. Chop tomato. Dice onion, chop garlic and cut corn kernels from cob.

2. In a heavy skillet, heat 1 Tbs oil over moderately high heat until hot but not smoking and sauté okra or squash with salt to taste, stirring occasionally, until browned, about 3 minutes. With a slotted spoon transfer okra to a bowl.

3. Add remaining Tbs of oil to skillet and add corn, onion and garlic. Sauté over high heat until it begins to brown, about 2 minutes. Stir and continue cooking for 2 minutes more until onions and garlic are soft. Stir in squash or okra, tomato and basil. Simmer, stirring occasionally, for 2 minutes, until everything is heated through.

4. Season with salt, pepper and lemon juice to taste.

SIMPLE FRIED OKRA

2 cups semolina, all-purpose flour, and/or cornmeal, in any proportions,	1 large egg beaten with ¾ cup milk or buttermilk
1 tsp salt	2 quarts oil for frying, peanut, corn, or canola
½ tsp pepper	1 heaping pint fresh tender okra
1 tsp dried thyme	your favorite vegetable dip

1. Whisk together the flour, salt, pepper and thyme. Prepare a batter by mixing just enough of the dry ingredients with the egg and milk to make a mix of pancake batter consistency.

2. Heat the oil in a large pot carefully, until a tiny drop of water spatters when added to oil. Lower the heat to medium. Roll the okra in the remaining dry dredge; dunk them into the batter, wiping off excess. Then re-dredge the wet okra in the dry dredge and place onto a plate. Fry about 8 or 10 at a time, raising the heat under the oil pot just before the frying begins. Okra is done about 15 seconds after they float.

3. Use a slotted spoon to remove the okra from the pot onto a drain rack or paper towels. Keep hot in oven until all okra is cooked, about 8 minutes maximum.

4. Serve with any good dip; Brett's personal favorites are vinaigrette and agrodolce (page 265). Julia prefers mayonnaise mixed with smoked paprika.

FRENCH ONION SOUP

4 Tbs butter
6 cups sliced onions
2 tsp sugar
1 Tbs flour
3 ½ cups beef stock, boiling
2 cups water
¼ cup Cognac or brandy

1 ½ tsp salt
½ tsp black pepper
12 slices stale French bread
1 ½ pounds Gruyere or Swiss cheese, grated

1. Melt butter over medium heat in a large sauce pan. Add onions and sugar, stir well, and cover. Cook, stirring occasionally, for about 20 minutes or until onions are wilted and golden. Cook onions for another 20 minutes, uncovered until they are a deep golden brown.

2. Add flour to the pan and stir well to fully incorporate flour into onions. Slowly stir in stock, water, Cognac, salt and pepper. Bring to a boil, reduce heat to a simmer and cook for 30 minutes.

3. Toast bread slices. Ladle soup into oven-proof bowls. Arrange croutons on top, sprinkle cheese on top. Put in oven, until cheese is melted and bubbly. Alternatively, melt cheese on top of croutons in the oven and then put them on top of the soup when serving.

TABOULI

This Mediterranean salad is a refreshing side dish to any grilled meat of fish.

½ cup fine grain bulgur
¼ cup fresh lemon juice
2 cups finely diced tomatoes
½ cup thinly sliced scallions
2 pinches of ground cinnamon
salt and freshly ground pepper

⅓ cup extra virgin olive oil
2 cups finely chopped flat-leaf parsley
2 Tbs slivered fresh mint leaves

1. Place the bulgur in a fine sieve, rinse under cold running water, squeeze dry, and soak in the lemon juice for 45 minutes. Use a fork to fluff the bulgur.

2. To the bulgur, add the tomatoes, scallions, cinnamon, and a few pinches of salt and pepper. Drizzle on the olive oil and toss. Mix in the parsley, and mint. Refrigerate for 1 hour, stirring occasionally.

MINTED PEAS WITH CUCUMBERS

1 Tbs butter

2 pounds English peas, shelled, or

1 pound snap peas

2 small cucumbers, sliced

½ cup chicken broth or water

2 Tbs fresh mint

salt and pepper to taste

1. In a large skillet, over medium heat, melt butter. Add cucumber slices and sauté for 2 minutes.

2. Add chicken broth and season with salt and pepper. Bring broth to a boil, and add peas cook just until peas turn bright green (approximately 2 minutes for shelled peas and 30 seconds for sugar snaps).

3. Remove from heat and stir in mint.

4. Serve as a side dish to lamb or grilled salmon.

PASTA WITH PEAS, MUSHROOMS AND SCALLIONS

1 pint fresh button mushrooms, portobellos or shiitakes

1 Tbs butter

2 Tbs olive oil

1 medium onion, sliced thin

2 cloves garlic, chopped

1 pound linguine, fettuccine or pasta of your choice

1 quart sugar snap or snow peas, or 1 – 2 cups of shelled English peas

1 bunch scallions, chopped

¼ cup parsley, washed and chopped

salt and pepper

1. Trim the mushrooms (remove and discard shiitake stems, if using). Slice ¼-inch thick.

2. Heat a large skillet over medium high heat. Add the butter and olive oil. Add the mushrooms, onions and garlic. Cook for 5 minutes, stirring every so often, until mushrooms are tender. Season to taste with salt and pepper.

3. Bring a large pot of heavily salted water to a boil. Add the pasta and cook according to the package directions. Two minutes before the pasta is cooked, add the English peas, if using.

4. Drain pasta and add sugar snaps, if using. Toss with mushrooms, scallions and parsley. Adjust the seasoning with salt and pepper.

PEAS WITH CARAMELIZED ONIONS

1 Tbs butter
1 Tbs olive oil
1 large onion, chopped
2 cups fresh shelled peas

1 tsp fresh thyme, stems removed
salt, pepper and lemon juice to taste

1. Heat a large skillet over medium heat. Add butter and olive oil. Add the onions and cook, stirring frequently for 10 minutes, or until they start to brown.

2. Add peas and fresh thyme, and a few Tbs of water. Cook until water evaporates and peas are bright green.

3. Season to taste with salt, pepper and lemon juice.

SUGAR SNAP PEAS WITH ONIONS, BLUE CHEESE AND WALNUTS

Unlike many spring vegetable dishes, this dish is excellent with red wine and red meats.

¼ cup walnuts, coarsely chopped
1 tsp butter
2 tsp olive oil
1 medium onion, sliced thinly
3 cups sugar snap peas or green beans

2 Tbs white wine
½ tsp salt
¼ tsp black pepper
¼ cup blue cheese, crumbled

1. In a large skillet, without any oil, toast the walnuts over medium heat, stirring constantly until they are fragrant. Remove from pan and reserve.

2. To the walnut pan, add the butter and olive oil. Sauté onions over medium heat until edges brown, stirring often. Add peas and sauté for 45 seconds (green beans should be cooked 1 - 2 minutes); add white wine, salt and pepper. Stir to make sure nothing is sticking to the bottom. Remove from heat.

3. Add blue cheese and walnuts; toss and serve.

BELL PEPPER, OKRA, AND TOMATILLO SALAD

This wonderful dish is essentially a "high summer" chilled succotash. Excellent on its own or to accompany grilled chicken or fish.

1 large red or green bell pepper, cut into chunks

1 Tbs olive oil

1 – 2 garlic cloves, chopped

1½ cups okra, cut into 1½ -inch pieces

1 – 2 cups ripe tomatillos

2 red peppers, sweet slender Italian slicing or bell

1 cup red cherry tomatoes, halved

2 Tbs fresh basil, lemon basil, or cilantro, chopped

1 cup cooked and drained black beans or navy beans

2 Tbs fresh lemon juice or any vinegar

salt and pepper to taste

1. Sauté the bell peppers in oil until soft. Remove these from the frying pan, but leave oil in pan.

2. Add chopped garlic and the okra. Sauté at high heat until the garlic barely browns, then remove from heat and let cool.

3. Meanwhile, peel and coarsely slice the tomatillos. Thinly slice the slender Italian peppers. Mix this together in a bowl along with the cherry tomatoes, the fresh herb and beans. Toss all together, then let sit 5 or ten minutes. Mix in the bell peppers and okra.

4. Add salt, pepper, and more vinegar or lemon juice, to taste.

GREAT STUFFED PEPPERS

6 medium-large peppers: cubanelle, Italian, or bell, red or green

1 tsp olive oil

½ pound sausage or ground beef

¼ onion, chopped

2 cloves garlic, chopped

3 ears of corn, kernels cut off

½ tsp salt

½ tsp black pepper unless the peppers are spicy

1 tsp whole cumin seed

½ pound (or more) grated cheddar or Monterey jack

½ bunch cilantro, chopped

1. Cut the shoulders off the peppers and remove the seeds and white tissue inside. Set the now ready-for-stuffing peppers aside.

2. Chop the white tissue and the meat from the pepper shoulders. Sauté this and the meat in a skillet with oil. When nearly cooked, add the onion and garlic and cook two more minutes. Add corn, salt, pepper, and cumin seed, and cook only 30 seconds more. Put into a large bowl and let fully cool. Then add the cheese and cilantro and mix well.

3. Stuff this into the peppers, and stand the peppers up in a small roasting pan (with sides). Bake for about 35 minutes in a 350°F oven, until the peppers are soft in all parts.

Excellent served with sour cream and more cilantro on the side, and a beer in the hand.

ROASTED RED PEPPERS WITH ARUGULA AND CHEESE

3 red bell peppers
2 cups arugula or mesclun, washed and drained
1 tsp red wine or sherry vinegar
1 Tbs olive oil
¼ cup freshly grated Romano,

Asiago or Parmesan cheese
fresh basil, shredded
salt and freshly ground black pepper

1. Blacken the skin of the pepper over a gas burner (or under a broiler) until blackened on all sides. Put in a bowl, cover with plastic wrap and let steam for 10 minutes. When peppers are cool, peel away blackened skin. Cut in half; remove and discard the stems, interior white membrane and seeds.

2. Put arugula on a large serving platter. Drape peppers on top.

3. Sprinkle with salt and pepper. Drizzle vinegar and oil on top. Sprinkle on cheese and basil.

4. This sensuous salad is meant to be eaten with a fork and sharp knife.

ROASTED PEPPER AND TOMATO SALAD

2 bell peppers, red or yellow   2 tsp balsamic vinegar
2 ripe tomatoes   2 tsp extra virgin olive oil
2 Tbs fresh basil   salt and pepper to taste

1. Blacken the skin of the pepper over a gas burner (or under a broiler) until blackened on all sides. Put in a bowl, cover with plastic wrap and let steam for 10 minutes.

2. Meanwhile, dice the tomatoes.

3. When peppers are cool, peel away blackened skin. Cut in half; remove and discard the stems, interior white membrane and seeds.

4. Cut the peppers into ½-inch wide strips. Mix with the tomatoes. Coarsely chop the basil and add to the peppers. Add the balsamic and olive oil. Season to taste with salt and pepper.

5. Let stand for 10 minutes before serving.

CHILES RELLENOS PICADILLO

Smoked duck is available at specialty food stores or through D'Artagnan.

¾ cup smoked duck breast or cooked free range chicken, chopped

¾ cup grated fontina or Monterey jack cheese

1 Tbs drained capers

1 Tbs chopped green olives

2 Tbs dried currants or raisins

½ tsp salt

8 fresh small bell or average sized poblano chilies

½ cup olive oil

1. Mix together all ingredients except chilies and olive oil.

2. Toss chilies with oil. Roast in 400°F oven until skin begins to turn light brown and blister, about 20 minutes.

3. When chilies are cool enough to handle, make a small incision (with a knife) along the side of the chili, in order to remove the seeds from the inside while still maintain the shape of the chili. Gingerly remove the seeds with a spoon.

4. Stuff the chilies with about ¼ cup each of Picadillo filling and return to roasting pan, cut side up. Return to oven to heat through before serving.

5. Serve with tomatillo salsa (page 237) and/or roast chicken and rice.

ROASTED STUFFED CUBANELLES

8 cubanelles or other stuffing peppers
1 Tbs plain oil
½ cup (leftover) cooked rice
1 cup raw or cooked corn kernels
½ cup grated Monterey jack cheese

tomato sauce (page 262)
salt and pepper to taste
OPTIONAL: jalapenos, basil, scallions, black beans, leftover cooked chicken

1. Toss peppers in oil and lay out in a single layer on a cookie sheet. Roast peppers at 400°F for 15 minutes or until the skin starts to blister and turn light brown. Take them out of the oven and let cool.

2. Meanwhile, mix together the rice, corn, cheese and any of the optional additions. Check seasoning for salt and pepper.

3. Cut the tops off the peppers and scoop out the seeds. Stuff the filling into the cavity of the pepper.

4. Return the stuffed peppers to the oven and bake at 375°F for 10 – 15 minutes.

5. Serve with tomato sauce.

OREGANO POTATO SALAD

Serve either warm, just after you've finished preparing, or cold. "New" potatoes are smaller spuds dug while the potato plant is still alive, and this makes new potatoes sweeter, nuttier, more tender-skinned, and with superior texture compared to older spuds.

½ onion, peeled and diced

1 red bell pepper, seeded and diced

1 garlic clove, minced

¼ cup balsamic vinegar

2 pounds new potatoes

¼ cup olive oil

¼ cup fresh mint

¼ cup fresh parsley

2 Tbs fresh oregano

salt and pepper to taste

OPTIONAL: black olives, pitted and coarsely chopped

1. In a small bowl, combine the onion, pepper, garlic, vinegar and pinch of salt.

2. Wash and cut potatoes into about ½-inch chunks. Put in a large pot and cover with cold water. Add a generous amount of salt (approximately 2 tsp per quart). Bring to a boil over high heat and reduce the heat to simmer. Continue cooking until the potatoes are tender, approximately 10 minutes. Test for doneness - a paring knife should insert easily into the potatoes.

3. Drain potatoes. Let cool slightly, and toss potatoes with onion mix, olive oil, (olives, if using) and fresh herbs. Season to taste with salt and pepper.

POTATO AND CHEESE GRATIN

This is a rich casserole that can serve as a whole meal if served with a good salad. No need to use fresh new potatoes; anything will do.

3 pounds potatoes, washed, not peeled, and sliced very thinly

2 cups milk, half and half, or cream (your choice)

5 medium-large cloves garlic, chopped

2 tsp salt

¾ tsp black pepper

1 onion, chopped

1 pound coarsely grated cheese: Cheddar, Gouda, Gruyere, Colby, etc.

1. Mix all ingredients together in a large bowl, then place into a 9-inch x 13-inch baking pan. With the back of a spatula, press down the potatoes so they lay flat and are submerged in the cream.

2. Bake at 340°F until tender all the way through, about 40 minutes. Test by inserting a butter knife into the middle of the dish. If it goes in easily, the potatoes are cooked.

3. Let cool for 10 minutes before serving.

ROASTED POTATOES WITH LEMON ZEST AND PARSLEY

1 quart new potatoes	zest from 1 lemon
2 Tbs olive oil	1 Tbs fresh parsley, chopped
1 Tbs corn starch	salt and pepper to taste

1. Preheat oven to 400°F.

2. Wash and dry potatoes. Cut into sixths, to yield about 3 cups.

3. Toss potatoes with oil, corn starch, salt and pepper. Make sure potatoes are evenly coated.

4. Place potatoes on a cookie sheet in a single layer. Roast in the oven for 20 minutes, or until crispy on the outside and tender on the inside.

5. Toss potatoes with lemon zest and parsley.

SIMPLE GARLIC-ROASTED POTATOES

This can be prepared using new potatoes or older ones, and are best using washed but not peeled spuds.

2 pounds potatoes, cut into 1-inch to 1 ½-inch chunks if too big whole

½ tsp salt

¼ tsp black pepper

2 Tbs olive oil

4 cloves garlic, peeled and chopped

OPTIONAL: 2 tsp chopped fresh rosemary, sage, thyme, or oregano

1. Mix the potatoes, salt, pepper, and oil; bake in a 350°F oven until just soft, stirring occasionally. Add garlic and bake until garlic starts to brown slightly. Add optional fresh herbs with the raw garlic.

2. A nice twist on this is to omit the other herbs but to squeeze ½ of a lemon, with some freshly chopped basil, when the garlic has just browned. Then roast 60 seconds more.

3. Leftovers are excellent served cold the next day, drizzled with vinaigrette.

SIMPLE SIMMERED NEW POTATOES

While these can be prepared with older spuds, they are truly sublime with freshly dug new potatoes. Be sure always to wash new potatoes gently, by immersing in cold water then rubbing any soil off, as the skins will too easily come off otherwise and are a required part of the new potato flavors.

2 pounds new potatoes, about 1 quart	¼ tsp black pepper
1 tsp salt	¼ cup butter
cold water to cover potatoes	OPTIONAL: 1 Tbs chopped fresh parsley, chives, or fennel leaf

1. Put spuds, salt, and water in a pot. Bring to a simmer. When fully cooked, a slender fork or knife will encounter little resistance when used to penetrate a few of the potatoes.

2. Drain off all but 2 Tbs of the water, add butter and pepper, and cooked another 2 minutes.

3. Stir in the optional herb(s), and taste again for salt and pepper.

TATER TOTS

4 medium potatoes	1 egg
½ cup grated Parmesan cheese	1 cup panko bread crumbs
½ cup all-purpose flour	1 cup clarified butter or canola oil
1 – 2 tsp salt	

1. Put potatoes in a pot and cover with cold water. Bring to a boil and cook potatoes until tender, about 20 minutes.

2. When potatoes are cooked, drain them and put them through a potato ricer. The ricer will extract the skin from the potatoes. Alternatively, you can grate the potatoes using a food processor or hand grater. In any case, grate the potatoes while they're still warm.

3. Let potatoes cool to room temperature.

4. Mix potatoes with Parmesan cheese, flour, salt (to taste) and egg. Be careful to not to over-mix.

5. Divide dough into 4 balls and roll potato dough into 4 logs. Cut each log into 1-inch pieces.

6. Roll each tot in panko bread crumbs. If you'd like, you can further reshape the tots to a round shape.

7. Heat a large skillet over medium-high heat. Add butter or oil. In batches, cook tots on all sides until evenly browned, about 5 minutes.

8. Serve with ketchup (page 261).

TRINIDAD CURRIED POTATOES AND CHICKEN

Mild and gentle; if you want more contrasts, add the chopped vegetables at the end.

1 tsp plain oil

1 large onion, minced

3 cloves garlic, chopped

2 tsp fresh ginger, minced

½ tsp crushed red chilies 3 Tbs madras-style curry powder

½ cup (or more) vinegar

3 - pound chicken, cut into 8 pieces

2 large potatoes, peeled and chopped

salt and pepper to taste

OPTIONAL: Chopped raw scallions, raisins, red peppers, cilantro and/or basil.

1. In a large sauté pan, heat oil. Sauté onions, garlic and ginger until they are soft. Add chilies and curry powder. Add enough vinegar to make a paste. Let cool.

2. Marinate chicken in paste for at least 2 hours, though overnight is ideal.

3. Barley cover chicken with water (approximately 1 quart) in a pot or large sauté pan. Add potatoes. Season with salt and pepper. Bring water to a boil. Reduce heat, and simmer for 20 minutes, or until potatoes and chicken are tender.

4. Garnish with optional ingredients, if desired.

STRIPED BASS WITH RADISH SALAD, SOY BEANS AND ORANGE GLAZE

This is adapted from Thomas Keller's recipe in The French Laundry Cookbook.

2 cups orange juice

5 Tbs butter

1 Tbs soy sauce

2 pounds Striped Bass, Arctic Char, trout or salmon filets

2 scallions, julienned

1 carrot, julienned

3 radishes or ¼ daikon, julienned

1 tsp lemon juice

1 Tbs olive oil

½ carrot, finely diced

¼ celery stalk, finely diced

¼ leek, finely diced

1 tomato, finely diced

½ cup fresh shelled soy beans (edamame), blanched

salt and pepper to taste

plain oil for cooking

1. Place orange juice in a pot, and cook over high heat until reduced to about ½ cup. Remove from heat and whisk in 3 Tbs butter. Season with soy sauce. Set aside in a warm place.

2. Combine scallions, carrot julienne and radish julienne in a bowl. Season with lemon, olive oil, salt and pepper.

3. Melt 2 Tbs butter over medium heat. Add carrot dice, celery and leek. Cook until soft, about 3 minutes. Add soy beans and tomatoes. Season to taste with salt and pepper.

4. Season fish with salt and pepper. Heat skillet over high heat, add plain oil. Cook fish on first side until brown and crispy, flip and cook for just a minute more on the second side.

5. Serve fish with orange reduction, small dice of vegetables, and the julienne salad.

ROASTED RADISHES WITH BUTTER AND SOY

1 bunch French breakfast radishes
1 Tbs butter

1 Tbs soy sauce
lemon juice to taste

1. Trim the fuzzy hair and leaves from radishes. Wash and cut into quarters.

2. Preheat the oven to 375°F.

3. Heat an oven proof skillet over medium-high flame. Add the butter. When melted, add the radishes. Cook for 3 minutes. Add the soy sauce, toss, and put the pan in the oven.

4. Roast radishes for about 5 minutes. Just before serving, squeeze a little lemon juice on top.

PASTA WITH FRIED SAGE AND PARMESAN

¾ pound pasta of choice
2 – 4 Tbs butter (depending on taste)
1 bunch sage, leaves picked

5 cloves garlic, sliced
¼ cup grated Parmesan cheese
½ cup chicken broth or cream
salt, pepper and lemon juice to taste

1. Cook pasta according to package instructions.

2. Meanwhile, melt butter over medium high heat in a sauté pan. Add sage leaves. Cook until they begin to look translucent and a little spotty. Add garlic slices. Continue cooking until garlic is lightly browned, about 1 - 2 minutes. Remove from heat.

3. When pasta is done, drain. Toss with sage and butter mixture. Add chicken stock and Parmesan. Stir to coat pasta. Season to taste with salt, pepper and lemon juice.

COCONUT – SORREL SOUP WITH SHRIMP OR CHICKEN

3 cups water

2 lemon grass stems, chopped

5 slices ginger or galangal

3 shallots or 1 large onion, peeled and coarsely chopped

3 – 4 hot chili peppers, chopped

4 Tbs lime juice

2 – 4 Tbs fish sauce

2 cups coconut milk

1 chicken breast, sliced thin, or ½ pound shrimp

½ cup sliced button mushrooms

1 bunch sorrel, coarsely chopped

2 sprigs cilantro, chopped

salt and pepper, to taste

1. Heat the water to boiling. Add the lemon grass, shallots, ginger and chilies. Reduce heat to low and simmer for 10 minutes and strain. Season to taste with fish sauce, and lime juice.

2. Return the broth to a pot. Add the coconut milk, chicken (or shrimp) and mushrooms. Simmer over medium heat for 5 minutes, or just until chicken is cooked. Stir in sorrel and cook for 1 minute more or until wilted.

3. Garnish with cilantro. Adjust seasoning with salt and pepper.

ROASTED SALMON WITH SORREL SAUCE

The bright acidity of sorrel makes it the perfect complement to the rich, buttery salmon. The sorrel loses its bright color quickly. You can purée the sauce with parsley or spinach leaves to bring green colors back.

4 6-ounce salmon filets	8 ounces sorrel (approximately 3 –
2 Tbs butter	4 cups, loosely packed)
1 small shallot or onion, peeled and diced	¼ cup cream
¼ cup white wine	salt and pepper to taste

1. Season salmon with salt and pepper. Set aside (in the fridge) until ready to cook.

2. Meanwhile, make the sauce. Coarsely chop the sorrel. Heat a medium-sized skillet over medium heat. Add the butter. When melted, add the shallots. Cook the shallots until soft, but not brown. Add the wine and cook until most of the liquid has evaporated (about 1 -2 Tbs remain). Add the sorrel leaves and stir until they wilt, about 3 minutes. Stir in the cream. Season to taste with salt and pepper. Set aside in a warm place until the salmon is ready.

3. Put salmon on a sheet tray, skin side down. Place under broiler for 10 minutes or until it the salmon begins to brown. Switch the oven to bake (375°F) and cook for 5 minutes more.

4. Serve salmon with sorrel underneath. Simple simmered potatoes (page 189) would be an excellent accompaniment.

FRIED ZUCCHINI WITH MINT

6 small zucchini	4 Tbs butter
2 Tbs all-purpose flour	3 Tbs white wine vinegar
1 egg, lightly beaten and mixed with 1 Tbs water	1 Tbs sugar
1 cup bread crumbs	1 Tbs mint
4 Tbs olive oil	salt to taste

1. Wash and dry zucchini. Cut into quarters. Season with salt to taste.

2. Dust zucchini with flour. Toss in egg wash, and coat in bread crumbs.

3. Heat pan over medium flame. Add oil and butter. Fry zucchini on all sides until bread crumbs are browned and crispy. Drain on a paper towel.

4. In a separate pan, heat sugar and vinegar, and cook until sugar dissolves. Stir in mint. Pour over zucchini.

5. Serve and enjoy.

SIMPLE SAVORY SUMMER MEATLOAF (OR MEATBALLS) WITH SPAGHETTI OR SUMMER SQUASH

This quickly made dish is very low-fat. The vegetables and herbs lighten the dish enough for enjoying even in summer, and flavorful free-range meat adds substantially to its healthiness. Serves at least six, with nice left-overs. Fifty minutes total to prepare and cook.

2 pounds lean, free-range ground beef or lamb

1 cup raw grated winter squash, summer squash or "forked" spaghetti squash

1 bunch mint, coarsely chopped

2 tsp salt

¾ tsp black pepper

3 cloves garlic, chopped

2 Tbs olive oil

TOMATO SAUCE

4 cups fresh diced beefsteak or cherry tomatoes

1 Tbs balsamic or red wine vinegar

2 cloves garlic, chopped

½ onion, chopped

¾ tsp salt

½ tsp black pepper

1 pint fresh basil, coarsely chopped

1. Mix first 7 ingredients together. Form into two loaves or many meatballs. Place in a roasting pan or cast-iron skillet, and drizzle olive oil over top. Broil on low broil setting until tops browns.

2. While meatloaf is broiling, quickly make the sauce by mixing the sauce ingredients in a bowl.

3. Once meat has browned, pour off most of the pan juices. Add the raw tomato sauce and broil until it too browns or slightly chars.

SIMPLE SUMMER SQUASH WITH GARLIC

5 small zucchini or summer squash
2 Tbs olive oil
4 garlic cloves, chopped
salt and pepper to taste
¼ cup white wine (optional)

2 Tbs butter (optional)
2 Tbs fresh herbs such as basil,
parsley or tarragon (optional)

1. Slice squash into ⅛-inch thick circles.

2. In a large skillet, over medium flame, add olive oil. Sauté garlic, the edges are barely browning, about 3 minutes. Add squash slices, ¾ tsp salt, and ½ tsp black pepper and continue cooking and stirring until squash has just softened, approximately 5 minutes.

3. Stir in any or all optional ingredients. Remove from heat and serve.

SOUTHERN STYLE SUMMER SQUASH

We also often add some fresh thyme and a splash of white wine, and really go for an excess of pepper, but the thyme and wine aren't really part of the Deep South tradition.

½ pound bacon, chopped coarsely, or 1 – 2 Tbs vegetable oil

1 onion, sliced

2 – 3 pounds summer squash, preferably a yellow variety, cut into quarter-inch half-moons

¼ tsp salt

½ – 1 tsp black pepper

1. If using bacon, cook in a heavy iron skillet or heavy bottomed pot until browning at the edges. Add the onions and cook until they brown slightly. Otherwise, simply sauté the onions in the oil until browning.

2. Add squash, salt, and pepper, stir generously, reduce heat to low, and cook, lidded, until the squash is very mushy. Ideally the squash browns a bit and sticks slightly to the pan bottom, but does not burn. Taste for seasoning again, adding salt and pepper if needed. The flavor should be slightly smoky, dominated by the sweetness of the squash and with a lot of black pepper.

3. This would typically be served alone, atop crusty bread as an American take on bruschetta, but more traditionally alongside roasted chicken, burgers, or steak.

SUMMER SQUASH CASSEROLE I

This recipe comes from Even' Star CSA Subscribers Don and Cindy Fletcher.

3 Tbs unsalted butter

1 pound summer squash thinly sliced (about 4 cups)

salt and freshly ground pepper

½ cup sour cream

1 Tbs fresh chives or scallion greens

¼ tsp paprika

¼ cup grated plus 2 Tbs Swiss cheese (or to taste)

3 Tbs fresh bread crumbs

1. Preheat oven to 375°F degrees. Heat butter in a large skillet over medium heat. Add the sliced squash, sprinkle with salt and pepper and sauté, tossing frequently, until golden (about 5 minutes).

2. In a mixing bowl, stir together the sour cream, chives, paprika, and 2 Tbs grated cheese. Add the cooked squash, stirring to combine ingredients, and transfer the mixture to a buttered, shallow baking dish, such as a 6-inch x 9-inch rectangular pan. Sprinkle the bread crumbs over the surface.

3. Bake 10 minutes; then scatter the remaining ¼ cup cheese on top and bake 5 minutes longer. Run briefly under the broiler till golden brown, about 1 minute. Serve immediately.

SUMMER SQUASH CASSEROLE II

This recipe comes from Julia's grandmother Charlotte Weil, a native of Montgomery, Alabama.

3 large or 6 small summer squash	¼ tsp cayenne pepper
1 ¼ cup milk	½ tsp pepper
2 Tbs vegetable oil	4 eggs, well beaten
1 Tbs flour	½ cup grated Gruyere or Swiss cheese
1 tsp salt	

1. Preheat oven to 400°F.

2. Dice the squash into ½-inch dice.

3. Pour oil in a heavy sauce pan and add the squash. Sprinkle with salt and pepper, cover and cook over very low heat, stirring from time to time until squash is soft and mushy.

4. In a mixing bowl combine eggs, milk, flour and cayenne.

5. Drain squash and add to egg mixture. Beat well with a rotary beater or whisk.

6. Pour into 2-quart buttered baking dish and sprinkle with cheese.

7. Bake 20 minutes or longer until top is brown and casserole is lightly puffed.

VEGETARIAN CUBAN SANDWICHES

Cuban sandwiches traditionally are filled with roast pork, ham, pickles and cheese. The roasted vegetables lend a meaty flavor and the chipotle peppers give a hint of smokiness.

½ cup mayonnaise
1 – 2 chipotle peppers (canned and packed in adobo), chopped, + 1 tsp adobo juice
1 red onion, chopped
2 Tbs fresh cilantro, chopped
2 Tbs oil
2 cloves garlic, chopped

1 carrot, peeled and sliced thin
1 yellow squash, sliced
1 zucchini, sliced
1 small eggplant, thinly sliced
1 French baguette
1 – 2 dill pickles, diced
¼ pound Swiss cheese, sliced

1. Mix mayonnaise, chipotle and its juice, cilantro and 2 Tbs red onion. Set aside. Toss eggplant with ¼ tsp salt.

2. Heat a large sauté pan over high heat. Add 1 Tbs oil. Add remaining onion and garlic. Cook for about 2 minutes. When the onions brown, add carrots and squash. Cook for another 2-5 minutes, or until the carrots are tender (the time may vary depending on the size of the carrots). You may need to add a little bit more oil, or water, to keep the vegetables from scorching. Remove veggies from pan and return to the burner.

3. To the same pan, add remaining oil and eggplant. Cook for 2 - 3 minutes, over high flame, until the eggplant is tender.

4. Meanwhile, slice bread in half and toast in oven.

5. When vegetables are cooked, remove from heat. Mix in pickles.

6. To assemble: spread a spoon of mayonnaise on each side of the toasted bread. Top one side with veggies, the other with cheese.

7. Bake in 350°F oven until cheese melts, about 4 minutes. Put the cheese side on top of the veggie side and press together. Cut into sandwiches.

ZUCCHINI STEWED WITH TOMATOES

5 small zucchini

2 Tbs olive oil

½ onion, sliced thin

4 garlic cloves

salt and pepper to taste

1 – 2 cups stewed tomatoes (see page 222)

¼ cup white wine (optional)

2 Tbs butter (optional)

2 Tbs fresh herbs such as basil, parsley or tarragon (optional)

1. Slice zucchini into ½-inch thick circles.

2. In a large skillet, over medium flame, add olive oil. Sauté onions and garlic, the edges barely browning, about 5 minutes. Add squash slices, ¾ tsp salt, and ½ tsp black pepper. Continue cooking and stirring until squash begin to soften, approximately 5 minutes.

3. Add the white wine and stewed tomatoes. Continue cooking as long or as briefly as you like; this is traditionally cooked until fully soft but need not be.

4. Stir in the butter and add the optional fresh herbs at the very end.

5. This is very nice served over pasta or rice, with grated Fontina cheese.

ACORN SQUASH WITH SUNFLOWERS AND DRIED CRANBERRIES

1 acorn squash, sliced in half lengthwise, seeded and then cut into 4 wedges per half
3 Tbs olive oil
1 lime, juiced

2 Tbs honey
3 Tbs dried cranberries
3 Tbs pepitas or hulled sunflower seeds
salt and pepper to taste

1. Preheat oven to 400°F.

2. Spread the squash slices on a cookie sheet. Toss with 1 Tbs olive oil. Season with salt and pepper. Roast for 20 minutes; then turn the slices over and roast for an additional 10 minutes.

3. While the squash are baking, combine lime juice, honey, remaining olive oil, salt and pepper. Mix well.

4. When the squash are cooked, arrange them on a serving platter. Sprinkle the dried cranberries and sunflower seeds all around. Spoon the dressing on top.

BUTTERNUT SQUASH WITH VANILLA AND CURRY

1 butternut squash, peeled, seeded
and cut into ¼-inch slices

1 tablespoon butter

2 tablespoons olive oil

½ vanilla bean or 1 teaspoon
vanilla extract

1 teaspoon Madras curry powder

salt and pepper to taste

1. Preheat the oven to 375°F.

2. Melt the butter with olive oil in a small skillet over medium-low heat. Add the curry powder and vanilla bean (if using). Let simmer for 5 minutes.

3. In a baking dish, combine the butter/curry mix with the squash (and vanilla extract, if using). Season to taste with salt and pepper.

4. Bake squash for 20 minutes or until tender.

BUTTERNUT SQUASH AND GINGER SOUP

If doubling this recipe, consider using two different winter squash varieties.

1 butternut squash	3 cloves garlic
1 onion	1 Tbs butter
1 celery stalk	8 cups water
1 carrot	½ cup cream (optional)
1-inch piece of ginger	salt and pepper to taste

1. Cut butternut squash in half. Roast in 350°F oven with a little water for 1 hour, or until tender (a butter knife will pierce the flesh easily).

2. Meanwhile, cut onion, garlic, celery, carrot and ginger into small pieces.

3. Heat soup pot over medium heat and add butter. Add onions, let sit until they begin to turn golden, add garlic, ginger, carrots and celery. Stir for 2 minutes.

4. Add water and salt.

5. When the squash is tender, scoop at the seeds, and discard. Scoop out pulp and add to soup. Purée.

6. Return soup to pot and simmer for 10 more minutes to let flavors blend.

ALTERNATIVE FLAVORINGS

This same method for squash can be used with different seasonings. Omit the carrot, celery and ginger and replace with:

a) 1 ½ tsp curry powder and 1 apple cored and chopped.

b) ¼ tsp each: cardamom, cinnamon and nutmeg.

CHILLED SPAGHETTI SQUASH & TOMATO SALAD

2 spaghetti squash, about 4 pounds

1 quart tomatoes

3 garlic cloves, minced

½ onion, peeled and sliced

1 – 3 Tbs balsamic or cider vinegar

1 Tbs olive oil

1 Tbs soy sauce

3 Tbs fresh basil, thinly sliced

salt and pepper to taste (about ½ tsp each)

1. Cut spaghetti squash in half and scoop out and discard the seeds and inner soft pulp with a large metal spoon.

2. Place squash face down on a plate and microwave about 2 minutes per half (multiple batches should be necessary) until BARELY soft. If you lack a microwave, steam for about 6 minutes until just soft. Let cool, then plunge a fork longitudinally through the inside flesh and work it from end to end to make the "spaghetti". Use a metal spoon to get out the last strands. Let cool to room temperature or cooler in the refrigerator.

3. Cut tomatoes into ½-inch chunks. Add tomatoes, onions and garlic to the cold squash strands. Mix in vinegar, olive oil, salt and pepper, soy sauce and fresh basil.

4. Taste and adjust for vinegar, salt and pepper.

HONEY ROASTED ACORN SQUASH

2 whole acorn squash
1 – 2 Tbs olive oil
salt to taste
1 stick (4 ounces) butter, room
temperature

½ cup honey
1 Tbs fresh thyme, minced
½ tsp fresh rosemary or sage,
minced

1. Preheat oven to 350°F.

2. Cut squash in half. With a large metal spoon, scoop out the seeds and discard. Cut each half into 4 wedges.

3. Place wedges in a baking dish and drizzle with olive oil. Sprinkle lightly with salt. Roast in oven for 20 minutes.

4. Combine butter, honey, salt, and herbs in a bowl and mix into a paste.

5. Remove squash from oven and spoon butter/honey mix all over squash. Return to the oven for 15 minutes, and bake until brown and caramelized.

SAUTÉED SPAGHETTI SQUASH WITH CAPERS AND GARLIC

This is excellent alongside seafood, beef or vegetarian beans.

2 medium spaghetti squash	1 Tbs capers
½ onion, peeled and sliced	1 Tbs butter
3 garlic cloves, chopped	2 Tbs white wine
2 Tbs olive oil	salt and pepper to taste

1. Cut spaghetti squash in half and scoop out and discard the seeds and inner soft pulp with a large metal spoon.

2. Place face down on a plate and microwave about 2 minutes per half (multiple batches should be necessary) until BARELY soft. If you lack a microwave, steam for about 6 minutes until just soft. Let cool, then plunge a fork longitudinally through the inside flesh and work it from end to end to make the "spaghetti". Use a metal spoon to get out the last strands.

3. Meanwhile, sauté onion with garlic in olive oil until just soft. Add capers, stir around, and then add spaghetti squash, 1 Tbs butter, and ½ tsp each salt and pepper, or to taste. Sauté for about 3 minutes more at moderate heat, then finish with white wine.

SQUASH GNOCCHI

Puréed blue hubbard squash would also be delicious in place of the butternut and/or acorn.

1 butternut squash	1 tsp salt
1 acorn squash	½ tsp baking powder (optional)
1 ½ cups all-purpose flour	1 cup chicken broth or 2 Tbs butter
2 eggs	
½ tsp curry powder	

1. Cut squash in half. Put on a baking sheet, cut side down. Add water to the pan, and bake at 350°F for 40 minutes or until squash are tender. It may be necessary to add more water to the pan if it all evaporates.

2. Let squash cool. Scoop out seeds and discard.

3. Scoop out pulp into a food processor and blend until smooth. Measure out one cup of purée (set aside the remainder for soup or another favorite recipe). Add flour, eggs, curry powder, salt and baking powder. Blend in food processor minimally, just until smooth.

4. Bring a large pot of water to a boil. Season with salt.

5. Fill a piping bag with a large plain tip. Fill with gnocchi filling. Gently pipe out ¾-inch logs, and then cut off into the water with a butter knife. Boil for 2 minutes. Scoop out with a slotted spoon into a dish with either the butter or chicken broth (this will keep the dumplings from sticking together before serving).

6. It may be necessary to cook the dumplings in batches.

Serve with Brussels sprouts, duck or turkey.

EASY WHITE PIZZA WITH SQUASH BLOSSOMS

Buy raw (pre-made) pizza dough or make your own.

TOPPINGS:

4 cloves garlic, chopped

½ onion, sliced thin

20 – 25 squash blossoms

2 – 3 cups grated mozzarella

¼ - ½ cup grated Romano or Parmesan cheeses

2 Tbs olive oil

½ tsp each salt and pepper

OPTIONAL: 2 Tbs fresh parsley or basil, or 1 ½ tsp dried basil or oregano

OPTIONAL: 1 cup chopped tomatoes

1. Pre-bake crust as per directions or your own experience to the just-golden-brown stage. Remove from oven and leave oven on.

2. Arrange the toppings on the crust, with the cheeses placed on last.

3. Bake at 400°F or broil very carefully until golden brown.

4. Excellent served with a chilled white wine, a lager or a pilsner.

STUFFED AND DEEP-FRIED SQUASH BLOSSOMS

This makes a great hors d'oeuvre, served with a tart dipping sauce such as Agrodolce (page 265).

1 Tbs olive oil

2 cloves garlic, chopped

¼ cup onion, minced

1 cup ricotta cheese

⅓ cup grated mozzarella

2 Tbs grated Romano cheese

1 large egg, beaten and divided into 2 bowls

½ tsp each salt and pepper

⅓ cup fresh basil, coarsely chopped

3 Tbs bread crumbs, semolina flour,

or coarse corn meal

20 squash blossoms, picked over to remove any stray insects

¼ cup milk

2 quarts (or more) peanut or corn oil

commercial chicken dredge or seasoned flour*

OPTIONAL: ½ cup minced ham, baby shrimp, or sweet corn kernels

1. Sauté the garlic, onion, and optional ingredients in the olive oil until the garlic has barely browned. Let cool.

2. In a large bowl, combine the three cheeses, onion-garlic mix, salt, pepper, basil, 1 bowl of (i.e., ½ beaten egg) egg, and the bread crumbs, corn meal or semolina and gently mix. Fill each blossom only 2/3 full with this mix (a tsp works best) and gently twist the petal tips to close; lay on a cookie sheet after stuffing.

3. Start heating the oil for deep frying. Prepare an egg wash by beating the reserved ½ egg with the milk in a medium-sized bowl. Dredge the stuffed blossoms into the commercial dredge or into a seasoned flour or cornmeal. Then carefully roll these in the egg wash and re-dredge in the dry floury mix.

4. When oil is hot (use a thermometer to read 350°F, or test by putting a wooden spoon in the oil - when bubbles vigorously form around the spoon, it is properly heated), deep-fry about 5 at a time, until they float; drain on paper towels.

5. Serve immediately.

* *To make your own seasoned flour: Mix 1 cup flour, cornmeal, or semolina, plus ¾ tsp salt, and ½ tsp each pepper and dried thyme.*

STRAWBERRY SALAD

A simple salad that lets the flavors of the strawberry sparkle.

1 pint strawberries	2 Tbs olive oil
1 bunch arugula, 2 cups mesclun or	salt and pepper to taste
1 small bunch watercress	1 Tbs red wine vinegar

1. Wash strawberries, cut out stems and quarter.

2. Put strawberries and greens in a serving bowl. Toss with olive oil to well coat the leaves. Sprinkle with salt and pepper. Finally, drizzle vinegar on top.

3. Serve immediately.

BASIC WHOLE BAKED SWEET POTATOES

Bake one 5-inch long sweet potato, or a similar chunk cut from bigger sizes, per person in a 340°F oven about 40 to 55 minutes, until a squeezed one is fully soft.

Note: Baking sweet potatoes in a pan will prevent the natural sugars from dripping onto the bottom of the oven and burning.

CHUNKED ROASTED SWEET POTATO WITH GARLIC

3 sweet potatoes (to yield 3 cups of chunks) or 1 quart of fingerling sweet potatoes, washed but not peeled
2 tsp olive or vegetable oil
½ tsp salt

¼ tsp black pepper
1 – 2 tsp chopped garlic
½ cup chopped onion
½ tsp fresh rosemary, sage or oregano

1. Cut potatoes into 1-inch chunks, skin-on (3 cups of chunks serves 3 or 4). Drizzle oil on top, and then stir in salt and pepper.

2. Microwave for 4 minutes, or skip this step and just roast in a heavy pan at 400°F until the edges start to soften. Add garlic, onions and herbs.

3. Lower heat to 350° F and continue roasting until garlic has slightly browned and sweet potato has softened, about 8-10 minutes.

SUMPTUOUS SWEET POTATO SALAD

This recipe comes courtesy of The Good Earth Natural Food Co., in Leonardtown, MD. This makes 8 - 16 servings, and is terrific left-over the second day.

DRESSING
- ½ cup extra virgin olive oil
- 2 Tbs pure maple syrup
- 2 Tbs orange juice
- 2 Tbs sherry or balsamic vinegar
- 1 lime, juiced
- 2 tsp minced fresh ginger
- ½ tsp ground cinnamon
- ¼ tsp nutmeg
- ¼ tsp cardamom

SALAD
- 6 pounds Beauregard or other orange variety sweet potato, peeled and cut into ¾-inch cubes
- ¼ cup olive oil
- 1 cup chopped scallions
- 1 cup chopped fresh parsley
- 1 cup pecans, toasted and coarsely chopped
- 1 cup raisins, brown or golden, or mix of both
- salt and pepper to taste

1. For the dressing, whisk the ingredients together in a small bowl. Season to taste with salt and pepper.

2. Toss sweet potatoes with olive oil, salt and pepper. Lay them on baking pans in a single layer and roast in a 425°F oven until tender, approximately 15 minutes. Let potatoes cool to room temperature.

3. Place sweet potatoes in a large bowl. Add scallions, parsley, pecans and raisins. Pour dress over and toss gently to blend. Adjust seasoning with salt and pepper.

SUPERB SWEET POTATO STUFFING FOR CHICKEN OR TURKEY

This delicious stuffing accomplishes 3 things: it adds (if using Japanese purple-skinned sweets) great chestnut flavor to stuffing easily and affordably; it adds more nutrition than any bread-based stuffing; and it provides a wheat-free stuffing fit for more diners (there are few if any who are allergic to sweet potatoes).

1 ½ to 2 pounds sweet potatoes, washed well but not peeled (Japanese purple-skinned is the preferred chestnut-flavored variety, but any high-quality sweets may be used)

1 Tbs olive oil

1 tsp salt

½ tsp pepper

½ – 1 pound high-quality pork sausage (optional) or 1 Tbs olive oil

1 onion, chopped

½ cup chopped celery (optional)

½ cup white wine or beer

2 Tbs fresh chopped herbs, preferably with some rosemary and sage (other herbs can supplement)

salt and pepper to taste

1. Cut the sweet potatoes into ½-inch chunks, place in a baking pan, toss with the olive oil, salt, and pepper, and bake in a 350°F oven until soft (approximately 30 minutes). Alternatively, you may microwave the chunks until just soft.

2. In a sauté pan, cook the crumbled sausage until fully cooked, then add the onions and celery and sauté until these are soft. If not using sausage, sauté the veggies in olive oil. Add the wine or beer and simmer another 30 seconds. Let cool, then add the fresh herbs and toss with the sweet potatoes. Taste for salt and pepper and adjust if needed.

3. A superior option is to mince the bird's liver and heart and add to the sautéing vegetables. This also substitutes for the pork sausage.

4. Generously salt and pepper the inside of a raw chicken or turkey and stuff it. Rub the outside as well with salt and pepper. Bake as per any other roast bird recipe.

SWEET POTATO FRIES

These are really easy, just like French fries. Assume 2 medium sweet potatoes will serve one hungry person.

1. Trim any bad spots from clean sweet potatoes but do not peel. Bake whole at 350°F until just soft (cooking too long will lead to hollow sweets that break apart upon frying). Let cool. At this point, the baked sweets can be refrigerated as is for up to six days before using.

2. To fry: slice each sweet potato into French-fry size strips, leaving the skin on. Deep-fry (see chapter for tips on deep-frying)until they float and have gotten a bit brown.

3. Drain, sprinkle with salt (optional) and serve. Good condiments are hot sauce (page 257) and ketchup (page 261).

SWEET POTATO LATKES

1 small sweet potato	1 egg
1 medium russet potato	1 tsp baking powder
1 onion	¼ cup plain oil
2 Tbs flour	salt and pepper to taste

1. Peel potatoes and onions. Grate using the largest hole of a cheese grater or food processor. Pour into a colander and squeeze out any liquid.

2. Mix potatoes with flour, egg, salt, pepper and baking powder.

3. Heat a large skillet over medium high flame and add about 2 Tbs oil. Spoon about 2 Tbs of batter per latke – about 4 latkes per batch. Cook for about 5 minutes or until brown, flip and cook on other side. Drain on a paper towel. Repeat until all the batter is used.

Serve with apple sauce (page 248) or sour cream or both.

SWEET POTATO VICHYSSOISE

3 Tbs butter	6 cups water
2 shallots, peeled and chopped	¼ cup cream
4 garlic cloves, chopped	2 ears corn, kernels cut off cob
2 leeks, white and light green parts, washed and chopped	2 chipotle peppers
1 celery stalk, chopped	1 Tbs red wine vinegar
1 sweet potato, peeled and diced	salt and pepper to taste
1 potato, peeled and chopped	OPTIONAL: chives or scallions, minced to garnish.
1 carrot, peeled and diced	

1. Heat pot over medium heat. Add 2 Tbs butter. Add ½ of shallots and garlic, all of the leeks and celery. Sweat for about 5 minutes. Deglaze with white wine.

2. Add potatoes, carrots and water. Simmer for about 30 minutes, or until potatoes are tender.

3. Purée soup. Add cream. Season to taste with salt and pepper. Chill soup.

4. While soup is chilling, heat a large sauté pan over high heat. Add remaining butter, corn, shallots and garlic. Sauté, without shaking the pan, for 3 minutes, or until the corn becomes sweetly aromatic. Season to taste with salt and pepper.

5. Purée chipotle peppers with ¼ cup water and 1 Tbs red wine vinegar.

6. When soup is chilled, garnish with corn and a drizzle of the chipotle purée. Sprinkle with chives, if you like.

VEGETARIAN/VEGAN BURGERS

2 Tbs olive or canola oil

½ cup minced onions

3 cloves garlic, peeled and chopped

2 cups cooked black beans, slightly mashed

¼ cup fresh oregano

1 tsp salt

¼ tsp cayenne

2 cups cooked sweet potatoes, mashed (preferably a mix of different varieties)

salt and pepper to taste

GARNISH: sour cream, cilantro and/ or cheese.

1. In a large skillet over medium-high heat, add 1 Tbs of the oil. Sauté the onions and garlic until just cooked. Immediately remove from heat.

2. Add the bean and oregano to the onions and garlic.

3. Sprinkle cayenne and salt on top of the mashed sweet potatoes. This helps to better disperse the seasoning.

4. Mix all ingredients together and chill for at least 45 minutes. Season to taste with salt and pepper.

5. Once chilled, form patties approximately 1 ½-inch thick and 4-inches in diameter.

6. Heat a large skillet over high heat, add remaining oil. Fry patties until golden brown and crispy on both sides. Flip gently, as these burgers don't hold together as well as meat patties do.

7. Serve with sour cream mixed with fresh cilantro, any cheese, or any condiment that you would normally serve with a beef burger. Best to serve with toasted crusty bread such as baguette or Kaiser roll.

BASIC STEWED TOMATOES

These tomatoes are the basis for many recipes in this book, and an excellent way to cope with a flood of ripe tomatoes. They also freeze exceedingly well as way to extend the summer harvest.

1. Remove any blemishes or rotten spots from fully ripe tomatoes. Wash, then chunk coarsely (you can leave cherry tomatoes whole, and should feel very free to mix many different kinds of tomatoes).

2. In a stainless pot, put tomatoes, 3 Tbs water, and about ½ tsp salt per quart of tomatoes. Bring to a gentle boil, stirring often, then reduce to a simmer and cook three more minutes. Let cool.

3. Using a colander, strain out but reserve the juice. This makes an outstanding tomato juice for pure drinking or Bloody Mary's. Freeze juice within 4 days; it keeps poorly.

4. The pulp remaining in the colander is rich in seeds, skins, vitamins, and tomato meat. If this amount of roughage is not to your taste, blend until smooth. Puréed or not, this forms the base for outstanding tomato sauces or tomato soups.

CARAMELIZED CHERRY TOMATO SAUCE

This recipe was originally created for Restaurant Nora in Washington, DC.

3 pints ripe or over-ripe cherry
tomatoes and/or cubed bigger
heirloom tomatoes

2 Tbs brown sugar

½ - 1 tsp fresh orange zest

fresh herbs of choice (but NOT dill)

1 Tbs minced garlic

2 Tbs minced onion

1 Tbs balsamic vinegar

½ tsp Kosher or sea salt

½ tsp black pepper

1. Mix together tomatoes, sugar, orange zest, ½ the fresh herbs salt, pepper, garlic and onions.

2. Attentively broil, not bake, in an oven until the skins of the top tomatoes have just blackened. Remove from broiler, and stir in other half of the above chopped herbs, or fresh herbs of your choice (not dill). Add balsamic vinegar, and taste for any further need for salt or pepper.

3. The sauce is outstanding served atop otherwise mundane chicken, fish, shrimp, or vegetarian rice dishes. It freezes well, but taste after thawing for additional herb, vinegar, or salt needs.

CHERRY TOMATO SALAD

Superb served alongside grilled meat, sausage or poultry. A serrated knife is the best tool for slicing the tomatoes. Two pints serves 6 as salad, and can easily be halved.

2 pints cherry tomatoes, halved

½ onion, very thinly sliced

1 clove garlic, finely chopped

½ bunch cilantro or basil, washed and chopped

½ tsp salt

½ tsp freshly ground black pepper

1 Tbs olive oil

lemon or lime juice to taste

OPTIONAL: ½ green or red bell pepper, thinly sliced in 1-inch strips

OPTIONAL: ½ cup pitted manzanilla olives, sliced

Mix everything together. Adjust seasoning to taste with lemon or lime juice.

GAZPACHO

On its own, this soup is a great way to start off a summer meal. You can give it an extra loving touch with Grilled Bread or Shrimp.

3 Roma or other plum tomatoes, coarsely chopped (optional: 1 smoked tomato)

1 heirloom beefsteak tomato, coarsely chopped

1 red onion, peeled and coarsely chopped

1 bell pepper, seeded and coarsely chopped

1 spicy chili pepper, coarsely chopped (remove seeds for a milder soup)

1 large cucumber, peeled and coarsely chopped

1 Tbs lime juice

1 Tbs lemon juice

1 Tbs red wine or balsamic vinegar

3 Tbs extra virgin olive oil

⅔ bunch scallion, diced

salt and pepper to taste

1. Purée first 6 ingredients in a blender.

2. Adjust seasoning with lime juice, lemon juice, vinegar, olive oil, salt and pepper.

3. Chill soup for at least one hour in the refrigerator. Taste for salt, pepper and acidity once more.

4. Garnish with scallions just before serving.

PANZANELLA

Recipes abound for panzanella. Most suggest that stale bread needs to be soaked in water and then squeezed out. We don't fully understand the purpose of this step -- obviously, the bread needs to soften up. But why not soften it in tomato juice?

1 large cucumber	fresh basil, chopped
1 tsp salt	2 Tbs extra virgin olive oil
2 large heirloom tomatoes	salt, pepper and lemon juice to taste
8 ounces fresh mozzarella	
2 cups cubed bread, stale or toasted	

1. Slice cucumbers. Toss with salt and let sit for 30 minutes.

2. Meanwhile, cube tomatoes and set aside in a small bowl. Cube mozzarella.

3. Drain excess water off of the cucumbers.

4. The tomatoes should start to give off water after 15 minutes of sitting. Strain this liquid and toss it with bread cubes.

5. Mix the remaining ingredients together just before serving. Adjust seasoning with salt, pepper and lemon juice to taste.

PASTA ESTIVI

This is another of the really light and healthy meals that match hot summer evenings. Estivi celebrates really good tomatoes and fresh basil or other herbs.

1 pound box capellini, fettuccine, linguine or other pasta of your choice

1 to 2 Tbs olive oil

4 cloves garlic, chopped

1 tsp salt

½ tsp black pepper

1 cup Genoa basil leaves or ½ cup fresh herbs of Provence, chopped

2 pints rainbow cherry tomatoes, halved, or 3-4 cups cubed heirloom tomatoes

salt, pepper and vinegar to taste

ON THE SIDE: grated Romano, Parmesan, or Asiago cheeses

1. Cook the pasta according to package directions and drain. While still very hot, add the olive oil, salt, pepper, and garlic; toss. Let cool.

2. When at about room temp, add the basil and tomatoes. Taste for final seasoning, and consider adding a splash of wine or balsamic vinegar.

PIZZA

Brett was taught to home-make pizza by his mother from age six onward. It was time-consuming but was one of the most welcome rituals of his entire youth, and he would still rather be in the kitchen with his Ma than almost anywhere else.

Creativity and "cleaning out the fridge" goals are best with this versatile dish. Any tomato sauce, or just olive oil, can be used. Cheese is a must: pizza without cheese is not pizza, it is focaccia. The cheeses can be mozzarella or Monterey Jack, plus Romano or Parmesan. We will also freely use odd bits of goat cheese, Asiago, Gouda, etc. The other ingredients can be extraordinarily diverse: zucchini, pre-blanched greens, green or black olives, pre-simmered new potatoes, fresh mushrooms, fresh basil, braised eggplant, meat or seafood of any type, fresh or roasted sweet peppers, even pre-cooked sweet potatoes or butternut squash. We like each pizza to have a focus (with only one to three ingredients), but we never make fewer than three different pizzas per batch. This recipe makes three medium pizzas.

THE CRUST

¾ cup white bread flour

1 cup warm water (about 90° to 98° F)

½ packet, or 1 tsp, yeast

2 ¼ – 2 ½ more cups bread flour

1 tsp salt

1 tsp olive oil

GREAT TOPPING COMBINATIONS

WHITE PIZZA:

Bell peppers and pre-cooked new potatoes

Summer squash and fresh basil

Greens, black olives, and garlic

Sweet red pepper, hot pepper, summer squash, and garlic

Chopped raw tomatoes, Genoa basil, and onion

Pre-baked garlic-infused butternut squash and basil

Arugula, garlic, and capers or anchovies

WITH TOMATO SAUCE:

Braised eggplant and any sausage or ground meat

Pre-cooked new potatoes and green olives

Braised eggplant and fresh Ancho or other spicy peppers

1. Prepare a sponge: mix the first three ingredients in a large bowl and let sit in a warm part of the room, stirring about twice in the first hour. The sponge is the baking term for a perfect environment for yeast to rapidly grow and multiply, and it is yeast that makes the dough light and flavorful. The sponge works best if you give it between 90 minutes

and 12 hours to work. You can make this in the morning before work, stirring only twice or thrice before departure, and then complete the dough when you get home. To complete, add the salt, oil, and bit by bit the flour. Add flour and knead until the dough doesn't leave many wet sticky bits on your worktable. Knead into a smooth ball, then cut this into 3 pieces. Lightly flour these and let rest while you get three pans ready by lightly sprinkling corn meal. Then use a rolling pin to roll out each piece of dough to the right size for your pans, often sprinkling more flour on your work surface to stop the dough from sticking. The dough will be fluffier if you press it out with your hands, omit the roller, and then work it out to the right size by gently stretching it with both hands and lots of flour.

1. Once the crusts are done, you must give them enough time to rise slightly, about 1 ½ to 2 ½ hours. Then bake as is in a 350°F oven until very lightly brown. This pre-baking makes for a crispier crust. If you prefer a doughy crust, let the dough rise but omit the pre-baking step.

2. These crusts may be made weeks ahead of time, baked and then stored frozen.

ASSEMBLY

3. Choose a sauce: any good tomato sauce, or olive oil for a "white" pizza. For pizza of this size, use about ½ cup tomato sauce or 1 Tbs olive oil per crust. Sprinkle with salt and pepper to taste. Then add your other ingredients. I like to have all the other ingredients I'm considering already chopped, in little piles, prepared while the crusts are rising. Beware too much loading of ingredients per pizza: sometimes less is more, and pizza cannot cook properly if it is too thick with vegetables et al. For crusts of this size, I'd use a maximum of ¾ cup total fillings per pizza.

4. For three pizzas we recommend 1 - 1 ½ pounds coarsely grated mozzarella and 6 Tbs finely grated Parmesan or Romano. Substitute other cheeses appropriately, but keeping a little mozzarella or Monterey Jack in a blend of more diverse cheeses keeps the cheese layer cohesive. Sprinkle the cheeses over the pizzas, then bake in a hot oven (at least 375° F) until the tops are medium brown, about 25 minutes. Let cool at least a few minutes before cutting and serving. Outstanding the next day, either cold or reheated.

5. Adjust all these amounts to your own tastes when you want to make pizza again.

RAINBOW TOMATO SALAD

This is a celebration of ripe, diverse summer tomatoes; store-boughts or out-of-season tomatoes will not work. A summertime must-have in fine restaurants that seek out local farmers. Serves about six.

1 – 2 pints cherry tomatoes, preferably of different colors

1 – 1 ½ pounds heirloom or very farm-fresh bigger tomatoes, preferably of different colors

2 tsp olive oil

2 tsp of your favorite vinegar

¼ – ½ tsp sea or Kosher salt

¼ tsp fresh ground black pepper

fresh basil or arugula if available

1. Pick a large wooden or china platter, chosen to maximize color contrasts between the tomatoes and the platter.

2. Cut each large tomato in half, then each half into ⅓-inch slices. Fan these slices in a thin layer on the platter. If you have red and other colored tomatoes, put the red ones down first to maximize color contrasts (gold or purple is lovely in the upper layers). Cut the cherry tomatoes in half, and place these in discrete groups, sorted by color, on top of or alongside the slices of bigger tomatoes. We try to have the most contrast and most height in the center of the platter.

3. Sprinkle salt and pepper over the tomatoes, then drizzle on the olive oil.

4. Right before serving, drizzle on the vinegar and sprinkle on the optional basil or arugula.

5. Excellent with a layer of freshly made mozzarella below the first slices of tomatoes. Appropriate wines to accompany this include a red Sancerre or Pinot Noir at slightly below room temperature, or a sangria, or a Portuguese vinho verde. The right starch would be crusty bread.

SMOKED TOMATOES

2 cups wood chips (hickory or apple is great, mesquite is okay) soaked in 4 cups of water or cheap white wine, for one hour

plenty of Roma or other plum tomatoes, cut in half.

1. Prepare a charcoal fire as you normally would on one side of the grill.

2. Drain the wood chips.

3. When the fire is on its last legs (there are still some red embers) get ready to move quickly: toss the wood chips on the fire. Put the grate on top, and place the tomatoes on the grate, ideally on the cool side of the grill and skin side down (should the skins burn, you can remove them; if the flesh burns, then cut it away). Cover the grill with the lid, open the vents only ½ way. Let the tomatoes smoke for 30 minutes or longer.

4. Purée the tomatoes for a sauce for lamb or steak, or add them to your favorite recipe for a little zip. They can be stored in the freezer or canned for long term preserving.

FOR A GAS GRILL:

Follow the directions as above; but put the drained wood chips in a disposable aluminum tray, and place it directly on top of the gas flame.

TOMATO BRUSCHETTA

1 pound ripe Roma or other plum tomatoes, chopped into ⅓-inch pieces

1 pound ripe cherry tomatoes, quartered, or heirloom tomatoes, cut into ⅓-inch pieces

¾ tsp Kosher or sea salt

2 or more cloves garlic, chopped

¼ tsp freshly ground black pepper

½ tsp balsamic or red wine vinegar

2 Tbs coarsely chopped basil

10 slices toasted bread, preferably from a baguette-type loaf

1. Mix the tomatoes and salt in a china, glass, or steel bowl. Let sit 30-45 minutes while you prepare the rest of your meal.

2. Put all into a colander to drain the juice. Mix in the other ingredients, add more vinegar, salt, or pepper to taste, and serve alongside the warm toasted bread slices.

3. An excellent way to start a summer meal when the weather is too hot to enjoy heavy meals or cooking.

TOMATO MOZZARELLA STRATA

Strata is a breakfast dish, similar to a quiche or frittata.

3 Tbs butter

4 slices bread

3 eggs

1 cup milk

½ tsp salt

3 Tbs fresh herbs: basil, scallions,
tarragon and/or parsley

1 Tbs finely diced celery

2 large tomatoes, sliced

8 ounces ball fresh mozzarella,
sliced

1. Pre-heat oven to 350°F. While oven is heating, melt butter in a 9-inch square Pyrex dish.

2. Lay bread slices on top of melted butter.

3. In a mixing bowl, combine eggs, milk, herbs and celery. Season with salt.

4. Pour egg mix over the bread.

5. Layer tomatoes, mozzarella and basil on top. Sprinkle with a little extra salt and pepper for seasoning.

6. Bake at 350°F for 45 minutes or until eggs are set. Serve immediately.

TOMATO SOUP

In the height of summer tomatoes, little embellishment is needed for this tomato soup. If you'd like, serve with a dollop of pesto (page 249) and a grilled cheese sandwich.

1 Tbs butter

2 garlic cloves, chopped

1 shallot or small onion, chopped

¼ cup white wine

4 cups diced tomatoes, a variety is good

salt and pepper to taste

OPTIONAL: ¼ cup cream

1. In a soup pot, melt butter over medium-high heat. Add garlic and shallots and cook for 5 minutes, or until soft. Add wine. Then add tomatoes and stock.

2. Simmer for 20 minutes. Purée.

3. Season to taste with salt and pepper. Stir in cream, if using.

EASY PICKLED GREEN TOMATOES

This is an "icebox" pickle, designed to be easy and require no canning. It's a great way to use up all the end-of-season tomatoes that won't have a chance to ripen on the vine.

tomatoes, whole cherry toms or 1-inch cubes of heirloom types, all green and underripe

½ cup Kosher or sea salt (not iodized salt)

8 cups water

1 – 2 chilies, to your taste, cut into 1-inch chunks

cider, red wine, or rice wine vinegar to cover (about 4 cups should be on hand, but likely won't all be used)

2 cloves garlic, sliced

1 Tbs pickling spice or a mix of coriander, fennel and cumin seeds

1 – 2 Tbs sugar (optional)

1. Put tomatoes in a large plastic, glass, or steel container.

2. Fully dissolve salt in water, stirring if necessary. Pour over the tomatoes. Refrigerate.

3. Place chilies in a clean jar, and cover with vinegar. Refrigerate. Leave both vessels alone for 7-14 days.

4. Pour salt water off of the tomatoes. Mix these, the chilies, and all other ingredients in a large bowl, return to the tomato container or to a quart Mason jar, and cover with new vinegar (more mild pickle) or the chili vinegar (more spicy pickle). Lid the pickle jar and return to the 'fridge. Let pickle at least a week before eating.

5. These pickles keep about 2 months before getting soft.

FRIED GREEN TOMATOES

3 green tomatoes
1 cup buttermilk, or 1 cup regular milk mixed with 1 Tbs sour cream or yogurt
½ cup flour
¼ cup corn meal

1 tsp salt
½ tsp black pepper
pinch or more of cayenne
½ tsp garlic powder
¼ tsp cumin
¼ cup plain oil or bacon grease

1. Slice tomatoes ½-inch thick and soak in buttermilk.

2. Mix together flour, corn meal, salt and other spices.

3. Heat a large skillet over a high flame. Add oil and/or bacon grease. When oil is hot, dredge tomato slices in flour mix and gently place in pan. Cook on both sides until brown and crispy.

4. Serve with rémoulade or red pepper salsa (page 99).

CHINESE TURNIP CAKES

This traditional recipe is often seen in Dim Sum houses, and is adapted from Florence Lin's Complete Book of Chinese Noodles, Dumplings and Breads. *This recipe easily halves or doubles. The recipe as we give it below, makes two loaf pans (9"x 4"x 3"). It is really easy to make, doesn't necessarily taste "radishy," and is absolutely delicious!*

3 pounds turnips or radishes

4 Tbs neutral oil

2 tsp kosher salt

½ tsp white pepper or ¾ tsp black pepper

4 cups rice flour

1 bunch scallions, chopped

2 Tbs neutral oil + 1 tsp dark sesame oil

OPTIONAL: ½ pound bacon or ground pork, precooked until edges are browned; then crumbled

GARNISHES: soy sauce, chili paste, minced scallions, hoisin and/or cilantro.

1. Wash roots well. Grate by hand or with a food processor.

2. Heat oil in wok or heavy-bottomed skillet; stir-fry the grated roots with oil for 1 minute on medium heat. Add the salt and pepper, cover and simmer over medium heat for 10 minutes, stirring often.

3. Meanwhile, line two loaf pans with plastic wrap.

4. Mix rice flour with 3 ½ cups water, then pour mixture into roots, stirring constantly. Cook an additional 3 – 4 minutes. Remove from heat. Stir in scallions and optional (but highly encouraged) meat.

5. Spoon mixture into loaf pans. When full, push down to remove air bubbles.

6. Steam these loaf pans in a wok or large pot with a steamer basket for 45 minutes. Check the water level regularly to make sure you don't burn the bottom of the pan.

7. Let cool in loaf pans and then refrigerate.

8. When cold, remove turnip cakes from pan and slice ½-inch thick.

9. Heat a skillet over high heat. Add second set of oil. Pan-fry until crispy on both sides.

10. Serve with garnishes.

SPICED TURNIPS

This is a great side dish for hearty roasted meat dishes, such as venison, beef or pork. You could also use rutabagas in place of the turnips.

2 Tbs mustard seeds

½ tsp allspice

½ tsp coriander

3 apples, peeled and diced - to yield 4 cups

1—2 large turnips, peeled and diced to yield 4 cups

3 Tbs plain oil

3 Tbs maple syrup or honey

1 Tbs parsley

salt and pepper to taste

1. In a large skillet over medium high flame, toast the mustard seeds until they start to pop. Add the coriander and allspice. Remove from the pan and set aside.

2. To the same hot pan, add half of the oil. Add the apples and cook until they begin to caramelize. Remove from pan and add to the mustard seeds. To that same hot pan, add remaining oil and turnips. Cook, covered, for about 5 minutes or until tender.

3. To the turnip pan, add the maple syrup and cook for a few minutes more. Return all the other ingredients back to the pan, and add the parsley.

4. Season to taste with salt and pepper.

JAPANESE NUKA BRAN PICKLES

Adapted from Wild Fermentation, *by Sandor Ellix Katz.*

This is a very traditional Japanese ongoing pickling technique, suitable for any and all root vegetables as well as larger collard, kale, mustard greens or cabbage leaves. They should be part of the repertoire of every pickle lover, and are served in the finest Japanese restaurants.

After fully immersing the fresh vegetables into the fermenting grains (the medium), push a piece of plastic wrap into full contact with the surface of the medium. This prevents unwanted fungi from colonizing the surface of the pickle. Once the pickles are at desired crispness and sourness, remove them from the liquid and rinse off the medium very, very well. Only then are they ready to eat.

EQUIPMENT:
ceramic crock or 2 gallon (minimum) Tupperware-type container
a dinner or dessert plate that fits inside above crock or Tupperware
a jar or Ziploc to fill with salted water to act as a weight
cloth cover

INGREDIENTS:
4 cups boiled brown rice (start with approximately 2 cups raw rice and 4 cups water)

1 ½ cup rice bran (health food stores will carry this)

three 4-inch strips dried kelp (sushi type is fine)

⅜ cup sea salt

½ cup miso

8 ounces beer or saké

1-inch piece of fresh ginger, cut into slices

about 10 small turnips, 6 large radishes, or 3 carrots

sea or Kosher salt and water, as needed

1. Toast the bran in a skillet until it slightly browns and smells nice, stirring often. Add to the cooled and cooked brown rice, and then mix all but the extra salt and water together. The vegetables should be immersed in the bran mixture and preferably not touching each other. If the blend is not as moist as prepared oatmeal, prepare a simple brine by dissolving 2 Tbs of the salt in a tepid two cups of water; mix enough of this into the crock to bring the medium to that "wet oatmeal" stage.

2. Place the plate atop the mix, and then weight this down with a jar filled with water or a Ziploc filled with brine. Cover with the Tupperware lid or (if a crock) a cloth. The mix should have a brine layer float to the top by the next day, partially immersing the plate. After two more days, remove the vegetables, clean and rinse as in the introduction, and taste them for sourness. If you like the whole package, add more

vegetables and continue ad infinitum. You should sprinkle the medium with Kosher or sea salt about every 8th or 10th batch, and consider adding more ginger and seaweed periodically as well. This culture is much easier to maintain in the winter months: summer vegetables and temperatures make it easier for microbes that are not Lactobacillus to invade.

MACOMBER TURNIP SOUP

Great on its own or garnished with scallions, tarragon and/or lobster meat.

1 recipe Roasted Turnips (page 244)

1 quart chicken stock or broth

¼ cup heavy cream

1 small leek, white and light green parts, cut and washed

salt and pepper to taste

1. In a large soup pot, combine turnip base, chicken stock and leek. Simmer for 20 minutes.

2. Purée in a blender (in two parts if necessary) until smooth. Add cream.

3. Return to pot to keep warm until ready to serve.

PICKLED TURNIPS

This recipe comes courtesy of longtime Even' Star CSA subscriber Sherry Jones. A great hors d'oeuvres for busy parties, or when heavier foods will later be served.

2 garlic cloves, sliced
thyme sprigs
½ tsp dried Greek oregano
1 bay leaf
2 tsp coriander seeds
2 tsp turmeric
1 tsp fennel seeds

½ tsp red pepper flakes
2 Tbs salt
2 cups water
½ cup cider vinegar
1 Tbs olive oil
1 pound small turnips, unpeeled, cut into wedges

1. Combine all ingredients, except turnips, in a bowl. Stir to dissolve salt.

2. Pack turnip wedges into a jar; pour in brine mixture. Screw on lid. Put jar on a shelf and turn it over every day for a week.

3. After a week, refrigerate.

ROASTED TURNIPS I

This approach has a deep European history and has recently become a staple in many of the better restaurants here in the US. The dish particularly complements heavier meat dishes, from Thanksgiving turkey to chicken or calves' liver to roasted beef, lamb, or pork. The mellow complexity of the roasted roots also adds unmatched character to vegetarian pasta or rice dishes.

3 – 4 cups baby turnips and/or rutabagas, washed, trimmed, but unpeeled

3 Tbs olive oil or neutral oil + olive oil blend

1 tsp salt

½ tsp black pepper

2 tsp fresh chopped thyme or rosemary, or 1 tsp dry rosemary (whole leaf, not powder)

1 Tbs chopped garlic

2 Tbs chopped onion

1. Cut any larger roots into pieces about 1 ½-inch long; leave smaller ones whole. Place in roasting pan, add salt, pepper, and oils, and toss around. Bake in a 350°F - 375°F oven, stirring occasionally, until only the very centers of the larger roots are still hard.

2. Add garlic, onions, and herbs, and continue roasting until all roots are just soft. Many will have begun to caramelize (i.e., turn brown, shriveled, and sweet). The roots cool quickly, so serve soon or in a lidded bowl.

ROASTED TURNIPS II

Serve as a side dish to braised short ribs, salmon or pork chops.

1 Macomber or other large turnip, to yield 2 – 3 cups diced

1 - 2 Tbs butter

1 tsp minced fresh ginger

1 tsp minced fresh garlic

1 crisp apple

salt and pepper to taste

1. Preheat the oven to 375°F.

2. Peel turnip and cut into ¾-inch cubes.

3. Melt the butter in a skillet over medium heat. Add ginger and garlic, and cook for 2 minutes, just to soften.

4. Toss the butter with the turnips. Season with salt and pepper. Spread them in a single layer on a cookie sheet and put them in the oven.

5. Roast the turnips for 20 minutes.

6. While they're roasting, core the apple and cut it into a ½-inch dice. Do not peel it.

7. After 20 minutes, add the apple to the turnips. Toss them together to make sure the apples get a little butter coating. Roast for 5 minutes more.

TENDER TURNIP VINAIGRETTE

Excellent as an alternative to green salads, or as a small appetizer preceding a heavy meal.

2 – 3 cups baby turnips or cubed rutabagas, washed, trimmed, but unpeeled

water to cover, in a lidded pot

1 tsp salt

any good salad dressing (page 269), or vinegar and oil

salt and pepper

1. Simmer the roots until just tender in the salted water (about 15 – 25 minutes). Drain. Let cool.

2. Add generous amounts of the salad dressing or drizzle with vinegar and olive oil. Season to taste with salt and pepper.

TURNIPS IN BUTTER

A nice comfort food for cold nights.

1. Cook the roots as in the above recipe, or in a chicken broth, but keep about a third of the simmering liquid in the pot once the roots are tender. Keep on a low simmer and add 1 Tbs butter, ¼ tsp black pepper, and (optional) chopped parsley.

2. Really good when you're not feeling so great. Goes very well with a baked potato.

TURNIP BRUSCHETTA

This recipe comes courtesy of Even' Star CSA member Jennifer LaRoche. She suggests serving it as an appetizer/hors d'oeuvre for a winter cocktail party or open house.

2 medium turnips
1 medium red onion
¼ cup (or less) olive oil
4 ounces prosciutto (optional)
1 – 2 Tbs balsamic (more or less depending on how much olive oil used)

1 Tbs fresh rosemary (or 1 tsp dried)
8 slices baguette

1. Dice the turnips and red onion.

2. In a medium skillet, heat olive oil over medium high heat. Add the turnips and onions and sauté for 10 minutes, or until onions or soft and turnips are tender.

3. Add the prosciutto (or ¼ tsp of salt) to the turnips, season with the balsamic vinegar and rosemary.

4. Toast the baguette slices.

5. Just before serving top each slice of baguette with turnip/prosciutto mix.

WATERMELON AND GOAT CHEESE SALAD WITH MINTY-CITRUS VINAIGRETTE

Extremely popular summer salad.

2 pounds watermelon (1 small, or portion of a large one)
2 Tbs fresh lemon juice
¼ cup extra virgin olive oil
2 Tbs fresh mint leaves

2 Tbs fresh basil leaves
½ pound mesclun or lettuce greens
½ red onion, sliced thin
4 ounces plain goat cheese or feta
salt and pepper to taste

1. Peel watermelon and cut watermelon into 1-inch cubes. Scrape out seeds.

2. To make the vinaigrette, combine salt, pepper, lemon juice and olive oil.

3. Chop mint and basil. Combine mint, basil and mesclun in a salad bowl. Add watermelon, red onion and crumble goat cheese on top.

4. Toss with the vinaigrette.

Sauces, Dressings and Vinaigrettes

APPLE SAUCE

When making apple sauce it's important to use baking apples such as Stayman or Ginger Gold. Empire apples also lend a lovely pink hue to the sauce when cooked with the skin on. When apples are mushy, pick out the skin and discard.

3 apples, peeled, cored and coarsely chopped
¼ cup sugar

½ cup water
a few drops of lemon juice

1. Cook apples, sugar and water in a sauce pot over medium heat, stirring until the sugar dissolves. Continue cooking over medium-low heat, covered, until apples turn mushy.

2. Remove from heat. Press sauce through a food mill, potato ricer or colander. Add a few drops of lemon juice.

BASIL OR ARUGULA PESTO

Pesto is a great way to use up vast quantities of basil or arugula, and freezes superbly. Arugula pesto, tossed with pasta and served with seared scallops, makes a great spring-time dinner. Basil pesto brightens any summer meal.

¼ cup olive oil

8 cloves garlic, coarsely chopped

½ tsp salt

¼ tsp black pepper

¼ cup white wine

¼ cup almonds or pine nuts, toasted and then cooled

about 4 cup arugula or basil leaves

at least ½ cup more olive oil or vegetable oil

¼ cup grated Romano cheese

more salt and pepper to taste

1. Sauté the garlic in the ¼ cup olive oil until soft but not very brown. Immediately add the next three ingredients and simmer until the wine volume has reduced by one half. Let cool.

2. Process all this in a Cuisinart until the garlic is fully puréed. Add the nuts and process until nearly smooth. Add the basil and PLENTY OF OLIVE OR VEG. OIL. Process further, until the basil is just barely smooth (no leaf pieces bigger than 1/8"), always adding more oil if the surface of the basil appears exposed to air. Add the cheese and process 15 seconds more. Taste for salt and pepper.

3. Place in a Tupperware or a glass jar and immediately be sure that there is at least ¼-inch oil floating over the basil.

4. The extra oil is intense and can be used for dressing salads. The surplus of oil in all stages keeps the basil from oxidizing to an unattractive black color.

5. Keeps 6 weeks in the 'fridge or 2 years in a freezer.

DREAMY GREEN GODDESS

¼ cup tarragon leaves, fresh

4 Tbs garlic chives, scallions and/or baby leeks, washed and chopped

½ cup arugula leaves or ¼ cup parsley leaves

½ cup mayonnaise

2 Tbs sour cream

1 tsp capers

½ tsp white wine vinegar

salt and pepper to taste

1. Combine herbs and greens in a food processor and process until coarsely chopped.

2. Add mayonnaise, sour cream and capers. Pulse machine until the mixture in just smooth.

3. Season with vinegar, salt and pepper.

SERVING SUGGESTIONS: Excellent as a sauce for rockfish/striped bass, grilled chicken, or grilled or blanched vegetables. It is also fabulous as a dipping sauce for fried okra, zucchini or eggplant.

HERB BUTTER

We usually make a large batch of herb butter and store it in the freezer. You can put a pat under the skin of chicken before roasting. You can also use it as a finishing touch for grilled salmon or steak; or toss steamed broccoli or asparagus with it.

1 Tbs fresh tarragon

1 Tbs fresh chives or scallions

1 Tbs fresh parsley

1 Tbs fresh basil

½ tsp whole fennel seeds

1 stick butter, room temperature

salt and pepper to taste

1. Chop herbs and fennel seed.

2. With a wooden spoon, mix herbs with butter. Season to taste with salt and pepper.

3. On a large piece of plastic wrap, roll into a log, wrap well, and store in the freezer until ready to use.

BEET VINAIGRETTE

This vinaigrette can be used for a salad or as a sauce for roast lamb or salmon. Sautéed portobellos served alongside would complement the vinaigrette, bringing out the sweet earthy flavors.

1 small beet, cooked until exceedingly tender

½ cup pomegranate juice

1 small shallot, peeled and coarsely chopped

¼ cup extra virgin olive oil

leaves from 1 spring of thyme

½ lime, juiced

salt and pepper to taste

1. Peel and chop cooked beet. Put in a blender with the pomegranate juice and shallot.

2. Being careful about splatters, pour in olive oil. Add thyme and purée for 10 seconds more.

3. Season with lime juice, salt and pepper.

BLACKBERRY-SAGE CHUTNEY

Serve this chutney alongside grilled polenta, steak or tuna.

2 Tbs bacon, finely chopped
¾ cup shallots, peeled and
chopped
4 Tbs blackberry or raspberry
liqueur
¾ cup blackberries

1 Tbs fresh sage, chopped
2 Tbs brown sugar
4 Tbs red wine vinegar

1. Add bacon to a dry skillet and cook over medium heat until lightly brown, about 5 minutes. Drain off excess fat, and add shallots. Cook for 5 minutes more or until shallots are soft.

2. Add liqueur and all remaining ingredients. Cook for 2-3 minutes, just to soften blackberries.

THAT EXTRA LOVING TOUCH:
While this chutney is great with plain grilled steak or tuna, you can enhance the meat by rubbing it before grilling with the following spice blend:

1 tsp black pepper
⅛ tsp star anise, ground
1 tsp salt
½ tsp cumin
1 Tbs chamomile (if you can't find it loose, just use chamomile from a tea bag)
1 tsp orange zest, grated

CILANTRO-LEMON MARINADE

For grilling rockfish/striped Bass, grouper, shrimp, chicken or turkey breast or, for vegetarians, zucchini, Chinese thick-stem mustard, tat soi or other heads of Asian mustards, pre-boiled potatoes or firm tofu. Marinates enough to serve four.

½ bunch cilantro	1 tsp black pepper
2 Tbs fresh lime or lemon juice	2 Tbs olive oil
1 ½ tsp chopped garlic	2 Tbs white wine or beer
3 Tbs chopped Egyptian onions or scallions	1 Tbs soy sauce
1 tsp salt	

1. Mix ingredients together in a bowl.

2. Marinate seafood or poultry for at least 2 hours. Vegetables should marinate for 45-60 minutes.

3. While the food is grilling, occasionally spoon some of the marinade onto it. Serve with freshly made salsa (mango, tomato, etc.) whenever possible.

VARIATION:

Substitute a Provençal herb blend for the cilantro, 1 tsp red wine or balsamic vinegar for the citrus juice, and 3 Tbs red wine for the white wine or beer. Use same marinating times as above.

CUCUMBER RELISH

¼ cup white or rice vinegar

2 Tbs sugar

1 small chili diced or ¼ tsp chili flakes (optional)

½ tsp salt

2 cucumbers, peeled (optional), seeded and diced

1 tsp sesame oil

GARNISHES: 1 Tbs scallions, chopped, and 1 tsp toasted sesame seeds

1. In small, stainless steel, non-reactive pot combine the vinegar, sugar, chilies (if using) and salt. Cook over medium heat, stirring constantly until the sugar dissolves. Let cool.

2. Toss cucumbers in seasoned vinegar and sesame oil; mix in garnishes.

GARLIC SCAPE – BASIL PESTO

Scapes offer all the flavor of garlic without the overpowering lingering taste of raw garlic.

¼ cup garlic scapes, chopped
¼ cup fresh basil
4 Tbs fresh lemon juice

½ cup olive oil
1 cup grated Parmesan cheese
salt to taste

1. Put garlic scapes, basil and lemon juice in bowl of food processor with steel blade, and process until scapes are very finely chopped. With food processor running, add oil through the feed tube and process 2-3 minutes.

2. Remove lid, add half of Parmesan cheese and process 2 minutes, then add the rest of cheese and salt and process 2-3 minutes more.

3. Serve with pasta, as a spread for crostini or as a condiment for grilled meat or fish.

MINT MOJO FOR LAMB OR SALMON

Mint and lamb are a classic pairing. This sauce is a fresh alternative to the classic mint jelly. It also work well with salmon.

½ cup coarsely chopped fresh mint
½ cup extra virgin olive oil
⅓ cup red wine vinegar

1 Tbs sugar
salt and pepper

1. Purée mint, oil, sugar and vinegar in a blender. Season to taste with salt and pepper.

2. This will keep for several days in the refrigerator.

ROASTED GREEN CHILI SALSA

This is excellent as a dip, or with rice, beans, eggs, chicken, mild fish, or pork.

1 – 2 pounds green tomatoes or tomatillos

2 Tbs olive or vegetable oil

4 cloves garlic, coarsely chopped

1 tsp salt

1 – 3 large mild green or red chilies (to taste)

1 onion, chopped

½ tsp ground cumin

¼ tsp ground coriander

2 Tbs chopped fresh cilantro

1 – 3 Tbs cider or red wine vinegar

OPTIONAL: ½ – 1 cup fresh, sweet corn kernels, and/or ¼ cup chopped red tomatoes

1. In an oven-proof skillet, mix green tomatoes (or de-husked tomatillos), 1 Tbs oil, garlic, and salt. Roast in a 400°F oven until soft and lightly browned. In a separate oven-proof dish, roast the chilies. This will allow you to adjust the spice level before committing the whole salsa to being too spicy. Let cool.

2. In a food processor, add the roasted green tomatoes/tomatillos and the desired quantity of roasted chilies, and process coarsely. You may also use a blender, but you may have to add some water or tomato juice to get the blending to start.

3. In a large skillet, over medium high flame, add remaining oil. Add the onion cumin, coriander, and optional corn and/or ripe tomatoes. Cook for three minutes, and then add the puréed green tomatoes and chilies. Simmer one minute, then let cool. Add cilantro and vinegar to taste.

4. Packed into a clean glass jar and lidded, this keeps only 5 to 14 days in the 'fridge. The salsa can also be canned, but freezing in plastic is the easiest long-term storage. If canning or freezing, you may have to add more cilantro upon opening.

ROMESCO

1 red bell pepper	4 garlic cloves
1 hot pepper	¼ cup olive oil
1 plum tomato	¼ cup sliced almonds
1 small onion or 2 shallots,	balsamic or red wine vinegar
quartered	salt and pepper to taste

1. Seed peppers and cut into quarters. Cut tomato into quarters.

2. Put all ingredients, except vinegar, in a shallow pot. Put in a 400°F oven until peppers begin to brown and almonds are toasted.

3. Pour off oil and reserve. Purée roasted veggies in a food processor. Drizzle in oil. Adjust seasoning with vinegar, salt and pepper.

JULIA'S HOT SAUCE

8 fresh red chilies (any variety available in the farmers' market)	1 large tomato
	1 – 2 Tbs canola oil
1 onion	¼ – ½ cup vinegar
1 bulb garlic	salt
½ red bell pepper	latex or nitrile gloves

1. Put on gloves before handling chilies. Remove the stems from the chilies. Peel the onion and cut into chunks. Peel the garlic. Cut the red pepper into quarters. Remove the stem from the tomato and cut into large chunks.

2. Toss the vegetables in oil and roast in a 375°F oven for 20 – 30 minutes or until the chilies are blistered and lightly browned.

3. Put everything in the blender and add just enough vinegar so that you can purée into a smooth paste/sauce. Season with salt.

4. Refrigerate, can or freeze.

HOMEMADE HOISIN (AKA PLUM SAUCE)

This is a superb way to use up very ripe peaches or plums; underripe fruit will not work. As such, it should be made during August. It will keep for many months, especially frozen, so make plenty to use throughout the year.

1 heaping quart very ripe plums, or
6 very ripe peaches, well washed
1 large onion, coarsely chopped
4 cloves garlic, whole
1 2–inch piece fresh ginger,
coarsely chopped

¼ cup soy sauce
1 Tbs dark sesame oil
dash sriracha or other hot sauce
cider vinegar to taste

1. Do not peel or pit fruit. Put in a deep non-reactive baking pan. Add onion, garlic, ginger and sesame oil. Mix together.

2. Bake plums or peaches at 350°F for 40 minutes, or until fully soft.

3. Add soy sauce and bake an additional 5 minutes. Remove from oven.

4. Once cool, remove pits. You may also remove the skins, but this is not necessary.

5. Puree in a blender or food processor until smooth. Starting with 1 Tbs increments of cider vinegar, add vinegar to achieve a brightly balanced flavor. Add sriracha to taste. Consider adding freshly minced ginger, as well.

RASPBERRY VINAIGRETTE

½ cup fresh raspberries
½ cup extra virgin olive oil
3 Tbs raspberry, sherry or red wine
vinegar

½ tsp fresh thyme
1 tsp sugar or honey
salt and pepper to taste

Combine ingredients in a blender. Purée until smooth. Adjust season to taste with either more salt, sugar, oil or vinegar. Will keep up to a month in the refrigerator.

BOLOGNESE SAUCE FOR PASTA

1 Tbs olive oil
1 cup diced yellow onions
4 cloves garlic, chopped
1 pound ground beef, ground chicken, ground pork or pork sausage, or leftover cooked poultry or beef (or any combination)
½ cup diced celery
2 tsp salt
1 tsp black pepper

4 cups chopped tomatoes or whole cherry tomatoes, puréed raw in the blender
½ cup dry red wine
1 cup heavy cream or plain yogurt
½ cup fresh basil, parsley or combination of both
OPTIONAL: mushrooms, eggplant or sweet peppers

1. Heat olive oil over medium heat in a large sauce pan. Add onions and garlic, stirring occasionally, until wilted and lightly browned. Add meat, breaking it up with the back of a spoon. Add celery, salt and pepper and continue to cook for 5 minutes.

2. Add tomato purée and wine. Simmer for 20 – 40 minutes until thick. Stir in cream or yogurt. Simmer 3 more minutes.

3. Adjust seasoning with salt, pepper and fresh herbs. Serve with pasta, or use for your favorite lasagna recipe.

HOMEMADE KETCHUP

6 cups diced tomatoes

1 Tbs plain oil

1 medium onion, chopped

4 garlic cloves, chopped

2 Tbs vegetable oil

¼ tsp cinnamon

¼ tsp ground allspice

½ cup brown sugar

½ cup cider vinegar

1 tsp salt

pinch cayenne

1. Purée tomatoes with juice in a blender until smooth.

2. Heat a stainless steel sauce pot (do not use aluminum because of the high acidity), over medium heat. Add oil, onions and garlic. Cook for about 5 minutes, stirring occasionally, until soft and lightly gold. Add spices and cook for one minute just to help them release their fragrance. Add the remaining ingredients. Turn heat to low and simmer for 1 hour, stirring occasionally, until the ketchup is very thick. Let cool.

3. Purée ketchup in blender until smooth.

Will keep for several months in the refrigerator.

MARINARA SAUCE

4 cloves garlic, chopped

1 onion, chopped

1 Tbs olive oil

salt and pepper to taste

4 – 6 cups stewed tomatoes (page 222)

¼ cup red wine

¼ cup fresh basil, coarsely chopped

OPTIONAL: ½ – 1 pound Italian sausage, 1 cup bell peppers, or button mushrooms, coarsely chopped

1. Sauté the onion and garlic in the oil until just soft. If using any of the optional ingredients, add them now.

2. Continue cooking and add the tomatoes. Simmer about 20 more minutes, then taste for salt and pepper, add the red wine, and resume cooking for 5 minutes. Remove from heat.

3. Let cool slightly, and then stir in the basil or any other herbs of your choice.

SLOW ROASTED TOMATO SAUCE

This is an easy recipe that tastes like a long-simmered sauce.

10 plum tomatoes, cut in half, lengthwise

2 shallots or 1 onion, peeled and coarsely chopped

6 garlic cloves, peeled and left whole

2 – 3 stalks fresh thyme

¼ cup olive oil

2 – 3 Tbs balsamic vinegar

salt and pepper, to taste

1. Toss tomatoes with shallots, garlic, thyme, and oil.

2. Roast the tomatoes in the oven for 30 minutes at 400°F or until tomatoes are tender and the garlic is lightly browned.

3. Purée the tomatoes, shallots, and garlic in a food processor. Adjust seasoning with balsamic vinegar, salt and pepper.

TOMATO COCONUT SAUCE

Serve this with a firm white fish. Before cooking the fish, season it with salt, fresh oregano and a big squeeze of fresh lime juice

1 Tbs plain oil	3 large tomatoes, chopped
1 – 2 garlic scapes or cloves, chopped	½ can coconut milk
1 jalapeno, chopped	salt, pepper and lime juice to taste

1. In a sauce pot, over medium heat, add oil, then garlic and jalapeno. Cook for 2 – 3 minutes or until aromatic and lightly browned.

Add the coconut milk and tomatoes. Bring to a boil, reduce to a simmer, and continue cooking for just a minute. Adjust seasoning with salt, pepper, and lime juice.

GREEN TOMATO JAM

2 cups brown sugar	6 garlic cloves, chopped
2 cups cider vinegar	1 – 2 jalapenos, chopped
6 cups chopped green tomatoes	1 tsp cinnamon
1 small onion, diced	
1-inch piece of fresh ginger, peeled and chopped	

1. Put sugar and vinegar in sauce pan. Bring to a boil, stirring until sugar has dissolved. Add tomatoes and remaining ingredients.

2. Simmer over low heat until chutney is reduced and thick, stirring occasionally, about 1 hour.

TOMATILLO SALSA

1 pound tomatillos, husked and washed

2 – 3 jalapenos

1 medium onion, roughly chopped

4 garlic cloves, roughly chopped

1 Tbs vegetable oil

¼ cup cilantro

⅛ tsp ground cumin

½ tsp cinnamon

⅛ tsp ground cloves

½ tsp sugar

salt to taste

1. Toss tomatillos, jalapenos, onion and garlic with oil.

2. Roast in 425°F oven until lightly browned and soft.

3. Purée in a food processor with remaining ingredients and approximately ½ cup of water.

4. Season to taste with salt.

AGRODOLCE

An ancient Italian sweet and sour sauce. Especially fitting for many vegetables, meat and poultry; not recommended for most seafood.

1 onion, minced
3 cloves garlic, chopped
2 tsp olive oil
2 – 3 Tbs brown sugar
4 cups good beef or chicken stock
½ cup red wine
pinch ground allspice

¼ tsp ground black pepper
½ Tbs fresh thyme, oregano and/or marjoram, finely chopped
salt, red wine or balsamic vinegar, to taste
OPTIONAL: 1-inch square of fresh orange or tangerine zest

1. In a stainless steel pot, sauté garlic and onion in the olive oil until just soft, about 3 minutes. Add brown sugar; once this bubbles, add stock, red wine, allspice, pepper and zest, if using.

2. Let simmer until reduced in volume by ¾; approximately 1 cup should remain.

3. Add fresh herbs. Simmer 4 more minutes.

4. Taste and add vinegar to taste, approximately 1 Tbs. Salt to taste.

Traditionally served warm or hot; great as a dip for fried vegetables.

BERRY VINAIGRETTE

Extra strawberry, blackberry, or raspberry jam can be used to make a superb salad dressing.

1 cup high-quality berry jam

2 Tbs oil

1 large onion, coarsely chopped

1 garlic clove

1 cup sherry, rice, red wine, or balsamic vinegar

⅔ cup olive oil or oil blend

1 Tbs fresh thyme or 2 Tbs fresh chervil

About 1 tsp each salt and pepper

1. In a heavy pan, carefully cook the jam until half-evaporated.

2. At the same time, sauté (in a separate pan and with the 2 Tbs oil) one coarsely chopped large onion and a garlic clove.

3. Blend all until smooth with the vinegar of your choice, the 2/3 cup oil, and the herb(s) and seasoning.

This dressing is suitable for all full-flavored salad greens and puts to shame the commercial raspberry dressings that are cloyingly sweet and weirdly thickened. A salad made with this dressing goes really well with a deep red wine like a syrah, petite syrah, shiraz, zinfandel, or cabernet franc or cabernet sauvignon. Quite appropriate when the winter winds howl.

GREAT CAESAR SALAD DRESSING

This recipe evolved to keep restaurant patrons really hungry for Caesar salads. Generally Caesar dressings are too bland, too fishy, too oily, too heavy, or too stale to enjoy. As a chef, Brett created this version and countless customers praised the bright, well-balanced flavors. Each ingredient listed is a necessary component.

Yield: approximately 3 cups dressing

2 Tbs peanut or corn oil

½ bulb (i.e., many cloves) garlic, chopped

½ cup white wine: any varietal will do except sweet ones

A Cuisinart or similar food processor (not a blender)

1 really fresh egg, large or extra-large, at room temperature

1 additional cup peanut or corn oil

1 cup olive oil

1 2-ounce can flat anchovy filets, packed in oil, or ½ tube anchovy paste (vegetarians could substitute ¼ – ⅓ cup capers)

¾ tsp black pepper, ground

1 tsp Kosher or sea salt

2 tsp Worcestershire or soy sauce

juice of 1 ½ large or 3 small lemons

¾ cup freshly grated Romano, Parmesan, or aged Asiago cheese

¼ tsp Tabasco sauce

2 tsp dried basil or ¼ cup chopped fresh basil or parsley

1. Sauté the garlic in the 2 Tbs oil in a heavy skillet. When garlic edges just begin to brown, add the white wine. Simmer about 4 minutes more, until wine has reduced volume by about half. Let cool.

2. Meanwhile make a simple mayonnaise: crack the room-temperature egg into the Cuisinart and run at high speed with the steel blade for 45 seconds, or until egg color is a pale yellow. Keep machine running, and very slowly pour in the two cups of oils in a thin stream (⅛" – ¼" wide). It should take about 45 seconds for the oils to be all added to the egg. You've now made unseasoned super-fresh mayonnaise.

3. Add the anchovies (plus their packing juices) to the mayonnaise; pulse 15 seconds. Add all other ingredients except the cooked garlic and the lemon juice; pulse until all are incorporated (about 30 seconds). Then keep the machine running while slowly streaming in the lemon juice and garlic fluids, followed by a fast addition of the chopped garlic.

4. Store in glass jar or plastic (never in metal).

5. Dress salad greens, especially more robust varieties such as romaine, watercress, tat soi or pac choi. A salad for four people would be about ½

pound of greens, 1 ½ - 2 Tbs dressing, about ½ cup seasoned croutons, and (optional) additional grated cheese, lemon wedges, 90-second soft-boiled eggs, or anchovy filets.

This dressing keeps usually keeps 4 months refrigerated, and is best after the first day.

LEMON-GARLIC-HERB DRESSING

This is especially good with cucumbers and summer squash

¼ cup freshly squeezed lemon juice (bottled juice won't work, so don't consider it)

¼ cup rice wine, cider or red wine vinegar

¼ cup extra virgin olive oil

¼ cup peanut or other neutral oil

1 cup loosely packed Provençal herbs or Genoa basil

2 Tbs minced sweet onion or fresh scallion

2 large or five small cloves garlic, peeled

1 tsp salt

½ tsp black pepper

3 Tbs Dijon or French country-style mustard

Place all these in a blender and process until just smooth. Refrigerate.

Also very nice with boiled, chilled potatoes.

ONE SIMPLE SALAD DRESSING

We prefer this dressing for tomatoes or mesclun

1 bunch Provençal herb mix or basil

5 cloves garlic

¼ cup chopped sweet onion or 2 scallion

1 cup balsamic, red wine or rice vinegar

¾ cup peanut oil or corn oil

¾ cup extra virgin olive oil

2 tsp salt or ⅓ cup soy sauce

1 tsp ground black pepper

1. Remove the tougher stems from the herbs, peel the garlic, and coarsely chop the onions or scallions.

2. Put everything in a blender and blend until smooth (less than 45 seconds). Pour into an old wine bottle, cork, and refrigerate.

Keeps practically forever. Shake well before using.

MARINADE FOR PORCINI AND PUFF BALL MUSHROOMS

Porcinis and puff balls must be marinated before grilling. This all-purpose marinade works for shiitake and wild mushrooms, squash, eggplant and bell peppers.

½ cup red wine

2 Tbs olive oil

2 tsp chopped fresh herbs, such as provençal blend, thyme, parsley, oregano, or any mix of the above

½ tsp salt

¼ freshly ground black pepper

1 Tbs balsamic or red wine vinegar

1. Toss ½-inch slices of porcini mushrooms, puff balls, summer squash, eggplant or quarters of bell peppers with marinade. Let sit 20 minutes for mushrooms or 40 minutes for vegetables

2. Attentively grill or broil over high heat until slightly softened.

REDUCED-CALORIE BALSAMIC VINAIGRETTE

A typical vinaigrette tames the acidity of vinegar with plenty of oil. The roasted shallots offer the same effect, thus reducing the amount of oil needed for a well-balanced dressing.

2 shallots or 1 onion	½ tsp salt
½ cup olive oil	½ tsp sugar
1 Tbs thyme	¼ tsp pepper
½ cup balsamic vinegar	

1. Peel shallots. In a small oven-proof pan or dish, mix shallots with ¼ cup olive oil. Cover with aluminum foil. Bake for 20-30 minutes or until soft, and nicely roasted.

2. In a blender, purée shallots, thyme and vinegar together. Slowly drizzle in remaining olive oil. Add 1 – 2 Tbs of water if it seems too thick. Season to taste with salt, pepper and sugar.

SUBLIME SALAD DRESSING

Great with cucumbers, and also good for a lunch salad of greens, broccoli, chick peas and sunflower seeds. Also great with sliced ripe tomatillos, or slices of avocado and onion.

¼ cup sesame seeds	½ onion, chopped
1 cup cider or rice vinegar	½ cup fresh mint
2 cups roasted (dark) sesame oil	½ bunch scallion
½ cup peanut oil	2 Tbs honey
½ cup soy sauce	2 Tbs white wine
2 Tbs raw ginger, chopped	1 medium egg
4 cloves garlic, chopped	

1. Toast sesame seeds in skillet until golden brown; cool 5 minutes.

2. Put all ingredients in blender; blend 30-60 seconds, until smooth. Taste; add salt and pepper as desired.

Keeps indefinitely if refrigerated.

DIPS FOR RAW RADISHES

For snacking, thinly sliced (but not peeled) radishes, turnips, and rutabagas are excellent dipped into soy sauce, hummus, or one of the following dips.

CURRY DIP

¼ cup plain yogurt or sour cream

1 tsp curry powder

1 Tbs minced raw onion

¼ tsp sea or Kosher salt

1 Tbs freshly squeezed lemon juice

cayenne and/or ground cumin, optional and to taste

Mix thoroughly. Keeps 14 days in 'fridge if covered.

SESAME-SOY SAUCE DIP

¼ c mayonnaise

1 Tbs sesame seeds, toasted and cooled

1 – 2 Tbs tamari or soy sauce

Mix thoroughly. Keeps 14 days in 'fridge if covered.

SPICY SALSA DIP

¼ cup plain yogurt or sour cream

2 Tbs good salsa

Tabasco or hot sauce to taste

salt to taste

1 Tbs chopped cilantro

Mix thoroughly. Keeps 8 days in 'fridge if covered.

Desserts, Sweet Treats and Beverages

APPLE TART TATIN

Tart tatin is a traditional French dessert that is cooked on the stove until the apples caramelize. This recipe simplifies the process without sacrificing the flavor.

8 apples, preferably Gala or Granny Smith	½ lemon
½ stick butter	pie dough
1 cup sugar	crème anglaise (or whipped cream or vanilla ice cream)

1. Peel and core apples. Cut into ⅛-inch slices. Line a 9-inch pie dish with apples. Squeeze lemon juice over apples and put pats of butter on top.

2. Add sugar to a pan with ¼ cup water. Bring to a boil, stirring until sugar dissolves. Continue cooking without stirring until the sugar turns a deep amber and caramelizes. Pour sugar over apples.

3. Drape pie dough over apples. Bake at 350°F until pie top is golden brown. Flip tart over onto a platter. Serve with crème anglaise.

PIE DOUGH

2 cups flour	1 ½ sticks butter, very cold
½ tsp salt	Approximately ¼ cup ice water
1 ½ tsp sugar	

1. In a large bowl, combine flour, salt and sugar.

2. Cut butter into 1 Tbs sized pieces , and add to the flour. With your fingers or a fork, combine the flour and the butter until the butter chunks are the size of peas.

3. Add just enough water to form dough. Do not over mix. Form into a ball that can stick together with only a few crumbs.

4. Let dough rest for 30 minutes in the refrigerator.

5. Roll dough ball out to ⅛-inch thickness. Chill again until ready to bake the apples.

CRÈME ANGLAISE

1 cup half -n- half	3 egg yolks
½ vanilla bean split or 1 tsp vanilla extract	¼ cup sugar

1. In a small pot, heat the half -n- half with vanilla bean (if using) just until small bubbles form around the side of the pot.

2. In a bowl, whisk eggs and sugar. Slowly pour hot half -n- half into eggs, whisking constantly and vigorously. Return mixture to heat and continue cooking over low heat until the custard thickens. This curdles easily so it is important to stir constantly and be attentive. Immediately remove from heat. If using vanilla extract, stir in.

BLUEBERRY BREAD PUDDING

3 cups whole milk
½ vanilla bean, split, or 1 tsp
vanilla
5 mint leaves
3 eggs
zest from one lemon
⅓ cup brown sugar
⅓ cup white sugar

3 cups stale bread, cut into cubes
1 tsp cinnamon
1 cup fresh blueberries
¼ tsp salt
butter
powdered sugar, blueberry and
mint for garnish

1. In a large sauce pot, combine milk, vanilla, mint, lemon zest and salt. Bring to a low simmer. Remove from heat and let stand for 15 minutes. Remove and discard vanilla bean (if using), mint and zest.

2. Meanwhile, in a large bowl, whisk together eggs and sugars. Whisk in the milk. Stir in remaining ingredients.

3. Grease a 9-inch x 13-inch Pyrex dish with butter. Pour in bread pudding batter. Bake at 350°F for 45 minutes.

4. Let cool for 10 minutes before serving. Garnish with powdered sugar, mint and blueberries.

BLUEBERRY CRISP

This recipe works with most fruit: apples, peaches, plums or blackberries.

FILLING
- ½ cup brown sugar
- 3 Tbs all-purpose flour
- 1 tsp grated lemon zest
- 5 cups blueberries
- ½ tsp cinnamon

TOPPING
- ⅔ cup rolled oats
- ⅓ cup brown sugar
- ¼ cup whole wheat flour
- 1 tsp cinnamon
- 3 Tbs melted butter

1. Combine filling ingredients, and spoon into an 8-inch square casserole.

2. Combine topping ingredients and spoon over filling.

3. Bake for 45 minutes at 375°F, or until top is brown.

BLUE MOON CARROT CAKE

This recipe is adapted from the Blue Moon Restaurant in Montgomery, Alabama. It's by far the easiest and best tasting carrot cake we've come across.

1 ½ cups neutral oil such as canola or grapeseed	2 tsp cinnamon
2 cups sugar	2 tsp baking soda
4 eggs, well beaten	2 tsp baking powder
2 cups flour	1 cup chopped pecans (or raisins or combination of the two)
½ tsp salt	3 cups peeled and grated carrots

1. Mix oil and sugar and beat well. Add eggs and mix well to combine.

2. Sift together dry ingredients twice and then add pecans (or raisins). Combine with above egg mixture.

3. Grease and flour two 9-inch cake pans. Fill pans and bake at 350°F for about 20 minutes. Cool.

4. Remove from pans and frost with icing.

ICING

1 8-ounce package cream cheese, room temperature	1 one-pound box confectioners' sugar
1 stick (4 ounces) butter, room temperature	1 tsp vanilla

Mix everything together with a wooden spoon or rubber spatula until well combined. Spread evenly on cooled cake with pastry knife or rubber spatula

NECTARINE PLUM CRISP

FILLING:
- ¼ cup brown sugar
- ¼ cup honey
- 3 Tbs all-purpose flour
- 1 tsp grated lemon peel
- 5 cups of sliced nectarines and plums (or apples or peaches)
- ½ tsp ground clove or allspice

TOPPING

- ⅔ cup rolled oats
- ⅓ cup brown sugar
- ¼ cup flour
- pinch nutmeg
- 3 Tbs melted butter

1. Combine filling ingredients and spoon into casserole a 9-inch square casserole dish.

2. Combine topping ingredients and spoon over filling.

3. Bake for 45 minutes at 375°F, or until topping is brown.

CLASSIC PEACH PIE

You may substitute store bought pie crust for this recipe. This recipe also works well with blueberries or strawberry/rhubarb.

PIE CRUST
- 1 ½ sticks butter, very cold
- 2 cups flour
- ½ tsp salt
- 1 ½ tsp sugar
- Approximately ¼ cup ice water

FILLING
- ¼ cup brown sugar
- ¼ cup white sugar
- 6 cups peach slices (peel peaches before slicing)
- 1 Tbs corn starch
- 1 Tbs lemon juice
- 1 tsp vanilla
- pinch salt

1. Make pie dough: Cut butter into 1 Tbs sized piece. Put in a large bowl with the flour, salt and sugar. With your fingers, combine the flour and the butter until the butter chunks are the size of peas. Add just enough water to form dough. Do not over mix. Form into a ball that can stick together with only a few crumbs.

2. Let dough rest for 30 minutes in the refrigerator.

3. Roll dough out to ⅛- inch thickness. Line a 9-inch pie pan with dough.

4. Make the pie and filling: in a large bowl, mix all filling ingredients together.

5. Preheat the oven to 375°F.

6. Spoon filling into prepared pie dough.

7. Place pie on a cookie sheet lined with foil or parchment paper (this will catch any drippings and keep them from burning on the bottom of the oven).

8. Bake pie for 40 minutes. Let pie cool for 15 minutes before serving.

GINGER POACHED PEACHES

1 quart water	1 cinnamon stick
2 cups sugar	4 slices ginger
½ lemon	8 peaches or nectarines
1 tsp vanilla extract or one vanilla bean, split	½ cup cream
6 whole cloves	¼ pound chocolate, melted

1. Combine water, sugar, lemon, spices and ginger in a pot. Bring to a boil.

2. Meanwhile, slice peaches in half.

3. Add peaches, and turn heat down to a simmer. After 2 minutes, remove skin from peaches. Cook for 15 minutes more, or until tender. Let peaches sit in poaching liquid until ready to serve.

4. Whip cream to stiff peaks.

5. Serve peaches with cream and a drizzle of chocolate.

THAT EXTRA LOVING TOUCH:

Make a crisp topping: Combine 1 cup oats, ¼ cup flour, 3 Tbs sugar, ½ tsp vanilla, ½ tsp cinnamon, and ½ cup melted butter. Spread out on a baking pan and bake at 375°F for 15 minutes or until crispy. Sprinkle on top of poached peaches just before serving and then finish with the whipped cream and chocolate.

PLUM (OR PEACH) PRESERVES

2 pounds ripe plums, halved and pitted

¼ – ½ cup sugar

½ cup water

1 (3-inch) cinnamon stick

1-inch slice of ginger (optional)

1. Coarsely chop plums and stir together with sugar, water, cinnamon stick and ginger (if using) in a 2-quart heavy saucepan. Simmer, uncovered, stirring occasionally (with a wooden spoon) until thickened and reduced to approximately 2 ½ cups, about 1 hour.

2. Discard cinnamon stick and ginger; and cool. Transfer to an airtight container and chill, covered.

PUMPKIN BREAD

1 ¾ cups all-purpose flour

1 tsp baking powder

1 tsp baking soda

¾ tsp salt

¾ tsp ground cinnamon

¼ tsp ground nutmeg

1 ½ cups pumpkin purée (see chapter 2 for technique)

½ cup sugar

½ cup brown sugar

½ cup vegetable oil + extra for brushing the pans

2 large eggs

½ tsp fresh ginger, chopped

¾ cup buttermilk or ¾ cup milk mixed with 1 tsp lemon juice

OPTIONAL: 1 cup raisins, 1 cup walnuts, and/or 1 cup pepitas (pumpkin seeds)

1. Preheat oven to 350°F. Brush two 9-inch loaf pans with oil.

2. Combine flour, baking powder, baking soda, salt, cinnamon, and nutmeg in medium bowl; whisk to blend. Mix in any of the optional additions. Mix pumpkin and both sugars in a large bowl until blended. Gradually whisk in oil, then eggs 1 at a time, then minced ginger. Stir in dry ingredients in 4 additions alternately with buttermilk. Divide batter among prepared pans.

3. Bake breads until tester inserted into center comes out clean, about 1 hour. Cool in pans.

PUMPKIN CRÈME BRULEE

yield: 8 custard ramekins

4 egg yolks

2 eggs

1 cup pumpkin purée

3 ounces brown or white sugar

1 pint heavy cream

¼ tsp salt

1 vanilla bean, split or 2 tsp vanilla extract

pinch of allspice

8 scant Tbs white sugar

1. Mix, do not whip, the egg yolks, eggs, pumpkin and brown sugar.

2. Heat cream with vanilla bean to scalding point (bubbles will form on edges). Gradually pour it into egg mixture, while whisking vigorously.

3. Add salt. Scrape seeds out of vanilla bean and add back to custard.

4. Pour mix into 6-ounce ramekins. Put ramekins in a water bath (2-inch high, 9-inch x 13-inch pan with 1-inch of hot water in it). Cover with foil.

5. Bake at 325°F for about 25 minutes, or until just set. (It's not a bad idea to check them after 20 minutes.) When shaking the brulees, they should look slightly loose in the center.

6. Cool.

7. Sprinkle about 1 Tbs of white sugar on top of each custard. Blow-torch the top until sugar is amber brown. Alternatively, place custards under the broiler and attentively watch until golden brown.

RASPBERRY PANCAKES

1 ½ cups all-purpose flour

1 tsp salt

3 Tbs sugar

1 Tbs baking powder

1½ cups milk

2 eggs, lightly beaten

3 Tbs melted butter

1 cup raspberries

½ – 1 cup maple syrup

butter for cooking as needed

1. Sift flour, salt, sugar and baking powder together into a bowl and make a well in the center.

2. Mix together milk, eggs and butter. Pour into well of dry ingredients. Mix until just incorporated.

3. Heat pan over medium heat. Add butter. Ladle in about 2 ounces of batter per pancake. Dot each pancake with a few berries. Cook for about 3 minutes. Flip, continue cooking. Serve immediately, or keep warm in a 200°F oven until ready to serve.

4. When finished making all the pancakes, add the remaining berries to the pan along with some maple syrup. Pour the berry-syrup over the pancakes just before serving.

MINTED BERRIES

1 pint strawberries, raspberries or combination
5 large mint leaves
1– 2 Tbs sugar (depending on the sweetness of the berries and your taste)

1 tsp vanilla or ¼ vanilla bean

1. Wash and hull the strawberries. Cut into quarters.

2. Cut the mint into thin strips.

3. Toss the strawberries with mint, sugar and vanilla. Let sit for 30 minutes (or as long as overnight) to let the flavors blend.

4. Serve with your favorite chocolate dessert or over ice cream.

SUMMER PUDDING

Essentially an uncooked bread pudding, laden with berries. You can use any berries you like – depending on what's available at your farmers' market or in your CSA share. Strawberries, blueberries and raspberries all work well in any combination.

6 cups assorted berries
¾ cup water
¾ cup sugar
1 ½ Tbs fresh lemon juice

16 – 20 ¼-inch-thick firm white bread slices
¾ cup chilled whipping cream

1. Combine berries, water, sugar and lemon juice in heavy large saucepan. Bring to simmer, and cook for 5 minutes, stirring occasionally. Strain berry mixture, reserving juices.

2. Line a 2-quart casserole dish with plastic, overlapping the sides. Trim crusts off of bread, making both squares and rounds (to better line the dish). Dip each slice into fruit juices. Place in bottom of dish. Dip 5 bread slices, 1 at a time, into juices; place around sides of dish. Spoon ½ cup berries into dish. Dip 3 more bread slices into juices. Place atop berries. Repeat process with bread rounds and squares, juices and berries to create another layer. Cover.

3. Place pudding on a rimmed baking sheet (to catch juices). Top with another baking sheet. Place heavy object on sheet to press down the pudding and help it set. Chill overnight.

4. Combine remaining berries and juices in bowl; cover and chill.

5. Beat whipping cream to soft peaks. Season if desired with 1 Tbs powdered sugar and ½ tsp vanilla. Unwrap pudding. Turn out onto a serving platter; remove plastic. Serve with berry-juice mixture, with whipped cream on top.

BALSAMIC GLAZED STRAWBERRY SHORT CAKE

½ cup sugar

¼ cup balsamic vinegar

2 quarts strawberries

½ cup heavy cream, whipped to stiff peaks

1. Put sugar in a sauce pan. Add ¼ cup water. Put over high heat, stir sugar to dissolve. Continue cooking without stirring for about 7 minutes or until sugar turns amber brown.

2. Immediately, add the balsamic vinegar (the sugar will harden). Continue cooking, stirring occasionally to help redissolve the sugar, until liquid is reduced by half. Remove from heat.

3. Just before serving, add strawberries. Serve biscuits with strawberries and cream.

BISCUITS

½ tsp yeast

⅔ cup milk

1 ¾ cup all purpose flour

1 tsp salt

1 Tbs sugar

2 tsp baking powder

4 Tbs cold butter

1. Dissolve the yeast in milk.

2. Combine dry ingredients. With a knife or fingers, cut the butter into dry mix. Mix in milk.

3. Roll out to ¼-inch thickness. Cut into desired shapes, e.g. 2-inch rounds.

4. Bake for 12 minutes at 450°F.

SWEET POTATO PIE

This recipe is adapted from that classic American kitchen aid, the Joy of Cooking by Irma Rombauer and Marion Becker, and we urge any of you that lack a copy to get one. Countless years of working in restaurant kitchens have left us still extremely appreciative of this simple but always useful text.

1 9-inch pie shell

1 ½ cups cooked sweet potato, de-skinned and mashed

1 ½ cups heavy cream or canned evaporated milk

½ cup brown sugar

¼ cup white sugar

½ tsp salt (omit if salt was added to sweet potatoes before baking)

1 tsp cinnamon

½ tsp dried ginger

⅛ tsp cloves, ground

4 slightly beaten eggs

1. Pre-bake a pie shell, homemade or store-bought, at 375°F until barely tan or brown.

2. Combine remaining ingredients with an electric mixer or by hand with a whisk. Pour into the pie shell and bake in a 325°F to 340°F oven until it sets, about 50 minutes. A slight shake should cause minimal waves in the filling. Let cool and serve.

VARIATION: An even lighter, more frothy pie can be had by separating the eggs into yolks and whites, whipping the yolks into all else, and whipping the whites separately to the soft peak stage. Then carefully fold the whites carefully into the rest of the filling and bake as above.

ZUCCHINI BREAD

2 – 2 ½ cups shredded zucchini
1 cup vegetable oil
3 eggs
1 tsp vanilla
¾ cup white sugar
¾ cup brown sugar
2 cups all purpose flour

1 cup whole wheat flour
1 tsp baking soda
¼ tsp baking powder
1 tsp salt
1 tsp cinnamon
1 cup chopped walnuts or raisins, or a combination of the two

1. Preheat oven to 325°F degrees.

2. Grease the insides of two 9-inch x 5-inch bread pans.

3. In a large mixing bowl, combine zucchini, oil, eggs, and vanilla. Mix thoroughly.

4. Add sugars to the above and mix until it is thoroughly blended.

5. In a separate bowl, combine the flours, baking soda, baking powder, salt and cinnamon. Whisk together to break up any clumps. Add the flour mix to the above. Mix until batter is well blended and even in texture. The batter should be smooth, except for the zucchini shreds. If it's not, add a few tablespoons of milk. Stir in the walnuts or raisins.

6. Divide the batter evenly between the two pans.

7. Bake for approximately 1 hour, or until bread is brown and springs back when gently pressed in the middle. Let cool for 10 minutes before serving.

PEACH SANGRIA

1 ½ pound peaches, peeled (optional) and sliced

⅔ cup sugar

2 cups apple juice

1 bottle dry white wine

3 Tbs Curaçao or other orange flavored liqueur

2 cups soda water (optional)

1. Combine fruit, sugar and apple juice in a pitcher. Stir to dissolve sugar and let sit for 1 hour.

2. Add wine and liqueur. Refrigerate.

3. Add soda water just before serving. Serve over ice.

BLOODY MARY'S

See Basic Stewed Tomato Recipe (page 222); the juice that is strained out of the stewed tomatoes makes this an amazing beverage. Makes one drink, though the recipe easily scales up if serving a crowd.

6 ounces of stewed tomato juice, chilled

¼ tsp salt

¼ tsp black pepper or dash of Tabasco

1 stalk fresh celery, cut into 8-inch x ½-inch strips (or ¼ tsp celery seed)

1 ½ ounces gin, vodka or whiskey

ice cubes

2 leaves fresh basil, lemon or Genoa

Assemble cocktail: put ice in glass. Add everything else and stir with the celery stalk.

One of the healthiest cocktails imaginable.

WATERMELON PURÉE

Good watermelon is not just for eating as a cut fruit. It is also excellent (after de-seeding) processed in a blender to make a purée for daiquiris, for homemade popsicles, or as the base for a sorbet. The purée freezes really well to enjoy in winter, when great watermelons are just a dream. Just pour it into a clean Tupperware, freeze fully, and then press 2 layers of plastic wrap over the exposed purée before tightly lidding with the Tupperware top.

1 large watermelon

1. Take rind off of watermelon. If the watermelon has seeds, remove them. Don't worry about the white, low-mass seeds.

2. Cut flesh into chunks that will fit into your blender.

3. Blend until just smooth.

FOR SORBET: use 3 cups of purée. Add 3 Tbs corn syrup or no sugar at all, the juice of 1 lime, and (optionally) 1 Tbs vodka. Put through an ice cream machine; re-freeze if necessary. Superbly healthy and refreshing!

MIXED DRINKS: not so healthy but delicious nonetheless. Blend 4 ice cubes, one cup purée with lime juice, pineapple juice, and a shot of rum or tequila. Serve over ice. For a lighter cocktail, mix 2 parts chilled Prosecco to 1 part chilled watermelon purée; serve in a champagne flute.

FREEZE POPS: Pour purée and nothing else into paper cups, leaving ½-inch of space at the top of each cup. Place the cups in a baking dish, cover tightly with a layer of plastic wrap, then poke a small hole in the plastic right over the center of each cup. Into each hole put a wooden popsicle stick (available at craft stores). The plastic wrap holds these sticks straight up. Freeze at least 24 hours. To serve, peel away the paper cup. Much healthier for beloved kids (or adults) than are factory popsicles.

Recipe Index by Ingredient

Broccoli Raab with Toasted Sesame Seeds and Ginger 68

Brussels Sprouts

Brussels Sprouts "Carbonara" 69

Quinoa with Roasted Brussels Sprouts 71

Roasted Brussels Sprouts with Balsamic and Olive Oil 70

Roasted Sweet Potatoes and Brussels Sprouts with Bacon and Sage 72

C

Cabbage - Green

Braised Green Cabbage with Apples 73

Ginger Sesame Bok Choy 131

Green Beans with Chilies and Lime 54

Halushki 77

Smoky Coleslaw 79

Thai Red Curry with Chicken and Vegetables 65

Cabbage - Red

Asian Red Cabbage Slaw 75

Braised Red Cabbage 74

Mexican Red Cabbage Slaw 78

Cabbage - White

Fresh Kim Chi 75

Cantaloupe

Cantaloupe Salsa I 80

Cantaloupe Salsa II 80

Fruit Salsa 81

Carrots

Beef Roulade with Cilantro Mojo 97

Blue Moon Carrot Cake 277

Caramelized Carrots with Honey 82

Carrot and Seafood Salad 84

Carrots in Butter 83

Cool Crunchy Cucumber Salad 106

Moroccan Style Beet Salad with Mint 60

Roasted Carrots 87

Smoky Coleslaw 79

Thai Red Curry with Chicken and Vegetables 65

Vegetarian Cuban Sandwiches 203

Vietnamese Meatballs with Crispy Salad 85

D

E

F

L

M

N

O

P

Peas

Peppers - Bell

Plums

Popcorn

R

Tender Turnip Vinaigrette 245
Thai Red Curry with Chicken and Vegetables 65
Turnips in Butter 245

S

Sage
Blackberry-Sage Chutney 252
Pasta with Fried Sage and Parmesan 194
Roasted Jerusalem Artichokes with Sage 159
Roasted Sweet Potatoes and Brussels Sprouts with Bacon and Sage 72

Scallions
Cilantro-Lemon Marinade 253
Cool Crunchy Cucumber Salad 106
Dreamy Green Goddess 250
Herb Butter 250
Pasta with Peas, Mushrooms and Scallions 176
Sublime Salad Dressing for Cucumbers 271
Sumptuous Sweet Potato Salad 216
Tabouli 174

Snap Peas
Green Beans with Chilies and Lime 54
Green Beans with Sesame Dressing 55
Sugar Snap Peas with Onions, Blue Cheese and Walnuts 178

Snow Peas
Green Beans with Chilies and Lime 54
Green Beans with Sesame Dressing 55

Sorrel
Carrot and Seafood Salad 84
Coconut – Sorrel Soup with Shrimp or Chicken 195
Roasted Salmon with Sorrel Sauce 196

Spinach
Baby Spinach Salad with a Warm Sherry Vinaigrette and Dried Cherries 150
Cauliflower – Spinach Soup 89
Chilled Spinach Salad with Sesame Dressing 151
Creamed Spinach 152
Korean-Style Spinach Salad 153
Swiss Chard and Ricotta Dumplings 155
Warm Frisée and Spinach Salad with Mustard Vinaigrette 135

T

W

Recipe Index by Course

Main Dish - Seafood
Carrot and Seafood Salad 84

Eggplant Parmesan with shrimp 119

Roasted Salmon with Sorrel Sauce 196

Spicy Shrimp, Celery and Cashew Stir-Fry 94

Striped Bass with Radish Salad, Soy Beans and Orange Glaze 192

Main Dish - Vegetarian
Arugula Soufflé 129

Chick Pea Crepes Stuffed with Wilted Greens 141

Classic Italian Greens and Garlic Soup 142

Coconut Curried Vegetables 145

Easy White Pizza with Squash Blossoms 212

Eggplant Curry 117

Ginger Sautéed Tat Soi with Tofu 156

Peas with Caramelized Onions 177

Pizza 228

Potato and Cheese Gratin 186

Potato and Jerusalem Artichoke Gratin 158

Quinoa with Roasted Brussels Sprouts 71

Roasted Stuffed Cubanelles 184

Savory Vegetarian Greens and Potatoes 148

Summer Squash Casserole II 202

Swiss Chard and Ricotta Dumplings 155

Swiss Chard Quiche 154

Tomato Mozzarella Strata 233

Vegetarian Cuban Sandwiches 203

Vegetarian/Vegan Burgers 221

Pasta
Bolognese Sauce for Pasta 260

Broccoli Raab with Sausage and Pasta 67

Brussels Sprouts "Carbonara" 69

Capellini with Chanterelles, Cream and Lobster 166

Fettuccine with Bacon, Greens and Sweet Corn 102

Halushki 77

Pasta Estivi 227

Pasta with Fried Sage and Parmesan 194

Pasta with Peas, Mushrooms and Scallions 176

Squash Gnocchi 211

Salads

Sauces, Vinaigrettes and Dressings

Side Dishes - Starchy

Snacks

Soups

About the Authors

JULIA SHANKS — chef and serial entrepreneur – developed a passion for cooking when she was 12 years old, cooking her way through the Time-Life Cookbooks. As a chef, she worked in restaurants around the country (including Restaurant Nora in Washington DC and Chez Henri in Cambridge), developing a taste for fresh, local and seasonal foods.

Julia received her professional training as a chef at the California Culinary Academy in San Francisco. She also earned her BA from Hampshire College and MBA from Babson College.

Today, Julia consults with restaurants, farms and food producers, helping them maximize profits and streamline revenues. She lectures on sustainable food systems and is the regional leader of Slow Money Boston.

In her tiny, urban garden in Cambridge, MA, she harvests vegetables seven months out of the year.

BRETT GROHSGAL has been the chef in 9 establishments and cooked in seven others, from New England to Louisiana to California and at sea, and over a twenty year period. Brett earned a Bachelor's degree in Botany from Berkeley and a Master's in Soil Science from North Carolina State University. As Brett's passion for cooking great foods evolved he began to grow his own produce and in 1996 he and his wife, Dr. Christine Bergmark, bought 100 acres of prime land in Lexington Park, Maryland.

Brett manages Even' Star Organic Farm for great foods, reliable harvests, and for respectful environmental stewardship. Brett and his treasured crew harvest crops year-round for restaurants, grocery stores, universities, and farmers' markets. The driving force of the farm since 2004 has been its CSA, which serves 200 families in the winter months and 350 families in the summer. Even' Star remains committed to the ideal that life is too short, and farm life too arduous, to ever grow or eat boring foods.

The Farmer's Kitchen is their first book and has received critical praise from The Boston Globe, The Boston Herald and Taste of the Seacoast.